DEHYDRATING YOUR FOOD

A SIMPLE AND EASY GUIDE TO DRYING YOUR MEATS, FRUITS, AND VEGETABLES FOR THE FUTURE

G.D. KASHUBA

CONTENTS

INTRODUCTION

How many times have you made it to the end of the day feeling overworked and too tired to cook? With the stress that you have dealt with and the responsibilities at home, it's too tempting to reach for the ready meals. But the fast food and ready-made meals come at a dire cost.

The American diet, one that is not solely consumed in the United States, can cause significant health problems and even shorten your lifespan. Because of the nutrition crisis, there are almost 900 deaths linked to poor diet per day in the United States alone (Aubrey 2022). That's more deaths than those caused by smoking. Known as the Standard American Diet, or SAD, we are at greater risk of chronic health conditions, including heart disease, stroke, diabetes, and cancer (Jakubiec 2023).

Aside from the physical effects of a poor diet, what you eat can also impact your mental health. Millions of neurons create what's known as the gut-brain-connection. Gastrointestinal issues or simply not providing the gut with the right foods can cause stress, anxiety, and depression. Serotonin, the happy hormone, helps reduce depression, and 95 percent of this hormone is produced in your intestine (Terry & Margolis 2017).

The worry about what we eat is often about obesity, and for good reason, but as you can see, what we eat can also affect mental and physical health. The scary thing is that not all these conditions are reversible.

What has gone so drastically wrong? Around 60 percent of the SAD is made up of processed foods, from soda to frozen meals and packaged foods. Sugar is another issue that lurks in so many foods, even those that are implied to be healthy. Overall, we eat approximately 19 teaspoons of sugar per day (Jakubiec 2023). To add to the problem, we are eating the wrong types of fats that increase bad cholesterol, and we don't get enough fiber, fruit, or vegetables.

There are several ways to improve your diet, but one that stands out from the rest is dehydrated food. Removing moisture from your food is both fun and cost-effective and, at the same time, highly nutritious. Nevertheless, this form of food preservation doesn't come without its challenges.

If you have started doing some research on dehydrating food, it's highly likely that you have come across a decent amount of resources, each with varying techniques. But then, all of a sudden, the next page you click on shows contradicting advice which leaves you confused. It's also more than possible that you discover information that is overly technical or information that has passed its sell-by-date! Food dehydration has evolved in recent years. It's not easy finding reliable information that reflects this.

Considering we are talking about your health, it can be unnerving to trust information that isn't 100 percent reliable. While dehydrating your food can increase nutritional value, it's essential that you get the process right and not run the risk of foodborne illnesses. This includes the daunting decision of what equipment to use. And, while we are on the subject, it's only natural that you are concerned about the time and financial investment that is required.

Sadly, these potential drawbacks are enough to put off some people, but for your own health, even the health of your family, you don't want to become one of these people. The solution is a surprisingly simple one, and it lies within the unparalleled **DEHYDRATE** nine-step framework.

Over the next nine chapters, you will embark on a logical journey that begins with **D**rying basics so that you understand the safety aspects and the science behind dehydration. Next, we will move on to the **E**quipment and methods so that you can make informed decisions. If you aren't looking to purchase a dehydration machine, you will also discover **H**ow to make your own dehydrator. In our chapter on **Y**ield optimization, we will go into detail on how to dry different types of food because it's not just about making beef jerky. Once you know what you want to dehydrate and how, you can experiment with **D**rying and long-term storage. In the chapter on **R**ecipes and applications, you will discover how diverse food dehydration can be. If that's not enough, you can take your food preparation to the next level with **A**dvanced drying techniques, **T**roubleshooting, and finally a fun chapter to **E**xperiment and enjoy.

Soon, we will take a much closer look at the health benefits of dehydrated food, but the **DEHYDRATE** method highlights numerous advantages to drying your own food. It encourages you to break free from the lure of fast and processed foods leading to greater sustainability. It can help you leave a positive impact on the environment. What's more, there is great satisfaction in opening your cupboard or pantry and seeing rows of food with a long shelf-life that you have prepared yourself. I'm no doomsdayer but I have extra peace of mind knowing my family has enough food in case of a crisis.

It wasn't easy reaching this peace of mind. Trust me, the **DEHYDRATE** framework wasn't born from a series of successes but rather a great number of mistakes. It was my own ups and downs, as well as experimentation, that sparked a passion to help others have smoother experiences with easy-to-follow steps.

Dehydrating your own food shouldn't be stressful and it shouldn't be boring, either. That's why this book has been created with objectivity in mind. I hope my experiences will guide you to success, but at no point feel it's what you must do. Buying or making your own dehydrator depends on your individual situation. If you want to switch one ingredient for something you prefer, go for it. I want dehydrating food to become a lifelong habit and for this, it must be something you love doing.

On that note, let's get straight into the first step of our **DEHYDRATE** method and discover why this is such a positive move in the right direction.

1

D—DRYING BASICS

"Cutting food waste is a delicious way of saving money, helping to feed the world and protect the planet."

— TRISTAM STUART

My interest in food dehydration didn't begin because of the health benefits. It actually started because of boredom. I was fed up with the same foods day in and day out, but the dried sections of grocery stores lacked inspiration—or were ridiculously expensive! The bigger picture, like nutritional value and cutting food waste, came along the way. If you have any doubts about drying your own food, by the end of this chapter, you will find your motivation.

DEHYDRATING FOOD SINCE THE DAWN OF TIME

Though there is an array of dehydrators on the market from the cheap and cheerful to the more sophisticated, humans have been using the sun to dry food since before we started to record history. The success of drying isn't based on sunlight and time alone. It requires a certain humidity, which is why the history of sun-drying food is richer in certain cultures.

Some of the earliest evidence goes back as far as 12,000 BCE in Middle Eastern and Asian cultures. There are archaeological sites in Egypt and Mesopotamia that show sun-drying has been used since 4,000 BCE. Drying fruit, vegetables, and fish gave the Egyptians a year-round supply of food, even during times of famine. In the Middle Ages, Romans built special houses to dry food, especially fruits, vegetables, and herbs. They included a fire in the houses for when there wasn't sufficient sunlight, and this would have led to smoked flavors too (Nummer 2002).

It wasn't until 1795 that two French inventors, Masson and Chollet, invented the first automated dehydration machine. The machine would heat food at high temperatures as well as extract the air, thereby vacuum sealing the food. This was one of the most pioneering events in the history of dehydrating food and became the groundwork for the modern dehydration process.

A lesser-known historical moment was the invention of spray drying, thanks to Samuel Percy in 1872. This technique was used to dry liquids with hot gas so that they became tiny droplets. The droplets were then passed to a drying chamber and exposed to hot air. As soon as the droplets came into contact with the hot air, the water content evaporated, and dry particles were formed. The benefits of Percy's invention weren't really noticed until the Second

World War when powdered milk was necessary for military personnel (Numanna Foundation n.d.). Spray drying is still one of the most commonly used techniques in the dairy industry today.

In 1906, food dehydration took another leap forward when Jacques-Arène d'Arsonval invented freeze-drying. Food was frozen, the pressure was reduced, and heat was added to remove the moisture content directly. This was a breakthrough because not only did freeze-dried food retain its nutritional value, but it also retained its structure. Freeze-drying isn't only used in the food industry. It's also used in the pharmaceutical and technological industries (Numanna Foundation n.d.).

Today, dehydrators and vacuum sealers are readily available, so this method of food preservation has expanded beyond commercial use. Dehydrated food and even meals are convenient for families whether that's at home or hiking and camping. Dehydrated food has a much longer shelf life and is easily transported, making it perfect for everything from space missions to emergency preparedness.

THE HEALTH BENEFITS OF DEHYDRATED FOOD

It's not enough to say that dehydrated food retains vitamins, minerals, and natural enzymes. To be completely reassured, you need to know precisely how this benefits your health. With this in mind, we are going to explore the wonderful world of antioxidants.

Your body naturally makes free radicals and antioxidants. Free radicals allow for cells to mature and support the defense system, but these molecules are unstable because they have an unpaired electron. Environmental factors, as well as processed foods, can increase the number of free radicals in the body, and this causes oxidative stress. Oxidative stress has been linked to cancer, cardiovascular disease, and neurological diseases such as Alzheimer's and Parkinson's disease (Pham-Huy et al. 2008). Antioxidants found in many foods, especially fruit, vegetables, and herbs, are generous compounds that donate an electron to a free radical and, therefore, make it stable.

To fully appreciate the antioxidant levels in dry food, let's look at some examples. Because dried foods are more concentrated, they have higher levels of oxygen radical absorbance capacity (ORAC), which indicates the amount of antioxidants. In general, apples have an ORAC of 2,573 without the skin and 3,049 with the skin. As soon as apples dry to 40 percent moisture, the ORAC levels increase to 6,681 (Haytowitz & Bhagwat 2010).

More than double the amount of antioxidants is impressive, but that's still nothing compared with herbs and spices. The ORAC for fresh basil is 4,805, but for dried basil, it increases to 61,063. Oregano is a powerhouse of antioxidants, with 13,970 fresh and 175,295 dried (Medindia 2021). Apart from the reduced risks of chronic health conditions caused by oxidative stress, dehydrated food also may improve your digestion. Research has shown that dehydrating food increases fiber, another element that is missing from our diets. You might even notice more energy when eating dehydrated food. Calories and sugar content are also concentrated during the drying process, but they are also more easily absorbed by the body, keeping you feeling more energetic for longer (WebMD 2022).

Dehydrating food means you can take advantage of these health benefits all through the year and not just when they are in season. Finally, in terms of health benefits, you know exactly what is happening with your food, so you know there are no chemicals or preservatives used. Organic food is not in everyone's budget. If you happen to fancy exploring the beauty of growing your own fruit and vegetables, you know that your food is completely organic and can be picked fresh and ready for immediate drying.

Speaking of budget, dehydrating food can save you plenty of money and relieve you of some of that financial stress you are under. Each food type will vary, but in general, your dried goods will last four years more than frozen foods and three years more than canned foods (Porter 2024). Since you don't need a fridge or a freezer to store dried food, you can cut down on your electric bill. More importantly, if there is any power outage, your dried food won't spoil. Take a look in your fridge and freezer and calculate how much you could lose if everything was spoiled!

I don't know about you, but kitchen clutter drives me crazy. I was forever wasting money on impractical storage items for food that would often be placed out of sight and forgotten. Drying and storing food helped curb this kitchen compulsion I had. With a little time, I had neatly organized shelves and saved a ton of space.

HOW DEHYDRATING FOOD CAN HAVE A POSITIVE IMPACT ON THE ENVIRONMENT

We can no longer wait for governments and large corporate companies to make the necessary changes to help save the planet. That's not to say that progress isn't being made but we as individuals must do our part as well. In the past I had the mentality of, "Oh, it's just one piece of plastic and I will recycle it anywhere," but I was once again missing the bigger picture.

Foods generally fall into one of four groups regarding the degree of processing. Unprocessed or minimally processed foods are raw; they go through processing, for example, crushing or drying, and are then packaged with no added ingredients. Processed ingredients like butter and oil should not be eaten alone, whereas processed foods have a mixture of ingredients and can be eaten alone. Sugar is a processed ingredient, whereas sugared nuts are a processed food. Ultra-processed foods are made with products you typically wouldn't use in your kitchen, such as preservatives and chemicals. It's not just the plastic used in all this processing; it's the environmental impact that all this processing causes.

One-third of all greenhouse gas emissions are generated by the world's food systems from processing, refrigeration, and transportation from farm to table. Ultra-processed foods are the biggest contributors. A report that reviewed 52 different studies found that this type of food made up a third of all diet-related greenhouse gas emissions, land use, and food waste. It also resulted in 36 to 45 percent of all diet-related biodiversity loss (Cliff 2022).

The production of ultra-processed foods relies on the mass production of crops like wheat and maize, often with chemical fertilizers and pesticides. This isn't doing our health any good. Above that, it's adding to soil erosion and land and water pollution. Recently, palm oil has been in the news for its potential disadvantages and the use of palm oil in ultra-processed foods has been linked to vast tropical deforestation (Warrell 2023).

Reducing your household waste is so simple with dehydration. Instead of leaving things to spoil, which we have all been guilty of, food can be dried and last for much longer. There is an additional benefit to saving you money. Each year, 60 percent of the $1 trillion in food waste can be traced back to households. On top of that, supermarkets waste 13 percent of food production (Englert 2024). Food that ends up in landfills decomposes and produces methane, a greenhouse gas 28 times as powerful as CO_2 at trapping heat within the atmosphere. It's estimated that 58 percent of methane emissions from landfills come from food waste (Environmental Protection Agency 2024).

I know it's a lot of facts and figures, but sometimes it's these real numbers that kickstart the essential action that is needed, so that everyone can have a positive impact on the environment.

IS DEHYDRATING FOOD SAFE?

The safety of home-dehydrated food is a huge concern. Dehydrated food in stores is often preserved with chemicals like sulfur dioxide, which provides some reassurance but defeats the purpose of dehydration if you are looking to reduce the chemicals and preservatives in your diet.

Dehydrating your own food is perfectly safe because you remove the water content from food. Microorganisms such as bacteria and fungi need water to survive. As soon as there is no moisture, there can be no enzymatic action, and food is preserved.

More care must be taken with meat because of Salmonella, E. coli, and other bacteria. Dehydrators use heat, but it's not safe to assume that this heat will kill bacteria. There is a risk that any bacteria in meat will become heat resistant with the gradual heating of a dehydrator. To safely dehydrate meat, precook it so that wet heat destroys any bacteria. Poultry should be cooked to 165°F and meat to 160°F (Hegerfeld-Baker n.d.).

Have you ever noticed that if you leave the lid of the sugar jar off, you end up with lumps in the sugar? Sugar is hygroscopic, meaning it has electronic properties that attract water. When the sugar concentration is high enough, it can literally suck out the water content of the bacterium through osmotic pressure, which essentially kills the bacteria (Wonderland Guides 2016). This is why dehydrated foods with sugar in them can last for so long and remain safe. Nevertheless, dried food should still be stored in clean jars, freezer bags, or containers with tight-fitting lids because not all foods contain sugar.

WHAT TO DEHYDRATE—AND WHAT NOT TO

We can't get this far and not mention one of the most popular dried treats throughout time—jerky! Although jerky is synonymous with the Wild West, the roots of striping and drying meat go back to the Egyptians. The word jerky comes from the Spanish "charqui," but jerky was easier for English speakers to pronounce. However, some believe that it comes from the Quechua word "ch'arki," meaning dry salted meat (Raging Bull n.d.). It was the cowboys and others who traveled for periods of time who began striping cuts of meat from bears, buffalo, and even whales to dry and make lightweight, nutrient-dense snacks for long journeys.

Aside from meats, fruit leathers are a great starting point. You can choose any fruit or combine different fruits and puree them. Once spread on a baking sheet, they can be dried and then cut into strips for a healthy snack. Fruit and vegetable chips are nutrient-dense, so eating them is a good way to get them in your five-a-day servings. Just remember that the sugar and calorie content will be higher compared with fresh versions, so don't get too carried away.

Soups are ideal for traveling, camping, or hiking because you have an entire meal in one package, and they are easy to rehydrate. There is no end to recipes when you start drying different vegetables and creating unique flavors. This is especially true when you add dried herbs and spices. You can also create entire meals by dehydrating legumes, grains, rice, and pasta.

Almost all foods can be dehydrated but you want to avoid anything that is high in fat. For safe and successful dehydration, moisture needs to be removed and fats don't evaporate. Personally, I recommend sticking to fruits, vegetables, grains, and cooked meats as a beginner. Once you have some experience, you can move on to things like dairy products and eggs, which require more attention to detail.

As much as you want to improve your diet and help the planet, don't forget to use your common sense. Some foods, such as tomatoes, pineapples, and apples, are easy to dehydrate, but if you can find offers in stores, especially organic offers, you can save both time and money on these deals. Don't put unnecessary pressure on yourself to dehydrate everything all at once. Over time, your pantry will fill up with amazing delights.

On that note, let's take a look at some of the best and not-so-great foods to dehydrate.

Good Foods to Dehydrate	Foods to Consider Dehydrating	Foods Not to Dehydrate
Fruits Vegetables Ground beef Ground sausage Sliced lunch meat Poultry Bacon Tofu Tempeh Herbs Spices Rice Pasta Legumes Sauces	Apples Apricots Cranberries Eggs Dairy products Fish	Fats Nut butter Avocados Olives Fatty meats Fatty nuts

This is by no means a complete list, as we would be here for a while, but it does show that there is a lot more to be dehydrated than just beef jerky. There will be plenty more types of food to dehydrate and inspire later.

With all the benefits of dehydrated food, it's no wonder you are keen to get started straight away. Before you start slicing away at your beef, ready to dry it, it's necessary to find out exactly what equipment you will need and even which drying method to use, all of which will be revealed in the next chapter.

2

E—EQUIPMENT AND METHODS

"Everyone wants to be strong and self-sufficient, but few are willing to put in the work necessary to achieve worthy goals."

— MAHATMA GANDHI

As we saw in the previous chapter, your intentions for dehydrating your own food may be varied. You might be hoping to improve your diet, prepare for a crisis, ease the strain on the planet, or a little of each. Regardless of your goal, anything worth achieving requires some effort. I found that in the early days, dehydrating took more effort than it should have due to my mistakes, which hopefully you will avoid. With time, the dehydrating process becomes second nature. So, let's begin by looking at what you can achieve with a dehydrator.

THE ESSENTIALS OF A DEHYDRATOR

A food dehydrator removes the moisture from food, reducing its size and weight while increasing its shelf life. With a combination of vents and fans, these machines circulate air at temperatures of between 104°F and 158°F over a longer period of time than traditional cooking. The temperatures and time mean moisture is successfully removed, but the nutritional content remains.

How long you need to use the dehydrator will depend on the type of food. Most foods will typically be fully dried in between four and 12 hours, although many machines can be left on for up to 24 hours (Mitchell & Cooper n.d.). There is no risk of over-dehydrating your food, but it's best to stick to the recommended times because unnecessary heat can start to reduce its nutritional value. It's not just the recommended time you need to pay attention to. The right temperature is also imperative for the best results, with higher water-content foods needing a higher temperature.

A common concern when looking at dehydrators is the cost. If you choose to invest in a commercial machine, how much you spend should be based on your needs. For example, size and features will play a significant role in the cost. A cheap and cheerful dehydrator can cost between $80 and $100, whereas more sophisticated machines can be more than $500, and commercial dehydrators run into the thousands.

It's not just the initial cost you should consider. You may think at first that your electricity bill will be sky-high because of the long periods of time dehydrators require, but these machines are highly efficient. The average stackable dehydrator can use between 500 and 1,000 watts (Dehydrated Foodz 2024). Meanwhile, the average oven can use between 2,000 and 5,000 watts (Marsh 2023). While researching machines, be sure to check the wattage and use your electric bill to calculate how much you can expect to pay to run the machine. Don't forget that while electricity cost is more difficult to calculate, you will be saving on food waste.

Dehydrators are incredibly simple to use. Most will have a certain number of trays, and it's helpful if they are removable so you can adjust the tray height for different types of food. There are normally just two settings: the temperature and the time.

You might also want to pay attention to the material from which the trays are made. Food-safe plastic, stainless steel, or Teflon-coated trays are far superior because materials like aluminum, copper, and other metals react with food. If the dehydrator is BPA-free (free from Bisphenol-A), it's a good sign. You may also want to make sure your trays are dishwasher-safe for added convenience.

RECOMMENDED DEHYDRATORS ON THE MARKET TODAY

In this section, we will take a look at the features of popular dehydrators you can find at the moment. This is an objective overview, and I am not endorsing one over the other, but it is helpful to get to know what is available that could suit your needs.

Excalibur 3900 9-Tray

This is from the deluxe range of Excalibur dehydrators and comes with a generous 10-year warranty. Between the nine trays, you have 15 square feet of drying space on polycarbonate trays. The overall dimensions are 12 inches in height, 17 inches in width, and 19 inches in depth. It weighs 24 pounds. Temperatures range from 105°F to 165°F. This dehydrator has a heavy-duty rear-mounted fan and a 600-watt heating element. There is a handy temperature guide on the top of the dehydrator, and it comes with a recipe book. There is no timer, just an on/off switch (Eartheasy n.d.).

Gourmia GFD1680

The exact dimensions aren't listed, but with six trays, it's a more compact dehydrator. The plastic trays are perforated for better airflow, but the dehydrator comes with protective food sheets for more delicate food as well as a drip pan to make cleaning easier, but the interior isn't non-stick. You will also receive a recipe book. It has an internal automatic fan, a top air vent, and a back air intake. The LED digital display makes this dehydrator easy to use. You can change the time and the temperature with a temperature range of 95°F to 158°F and 480 watts (Best Buy n.d.).

NESCO Gardenmaster Pro

The first thing you would notice is that it isn't the best-looking dehydrator. It's off-white and round (16 x 16 x 11 inches). Although it only weighs 11 pounds, it might be a little awkward to store in cupboards. It comes with four trays, but you can buy additional trays and stack up to 20. The trays don't lock together, so if you need to move the unit, be sure to pick it up from the bottom. The trays are sturdy plastic and dishwasher safe. As the fan is top-mounted, there's little mess, and it's an easy dehydrator to clean. What sets this dehydrator apart from the others is the temperature control. The 1,000-watt motor allows for a temperature range of 90°F to 160°F, with a timer for up to 48 hours. The efficiency of the machine means you will rarely need to set the timer for that long (Melynn 2023).

Cosori Premium

There are two versions: the six-tray and the 10-tray. We will focus on the six-tray for its more compact size at 17.8 x 13.5 x 12.2

inches and 6.48 square feet of drying space. The trays are stainless steel and fit in most dishwashers. It only comes with two tray liners and one fruit leather sheet. There is an excellent range of settings from 95°F to 165°F and 30 minutes to 48 hours, all set through the touch-control LED display. This dehydrator is 600 watts, and a great feature is the overheating protection, so it will automatically switch off when it gets too hot (Baldwin 2024).

Magic Mill MFD-7700

It's a slightly pricier dehydrator but comes with features to warrant the additional investment. It looks stunning and is just 15.5 x 11.5 x 10.25 inches. With seven stainless steel trays, you can dehydrate up to eight pounds of food at once. The trays are dishwasher safe, and all parts of the dehydrator are made with food-grade BPA-free material. Another safety feature is the overheat protection. Temperatures can be set between 95°F and 167°F. The timer is between 30 minutes and 24 hours. It also comes with a countdown timer on the digital touchscreen. It's just 480 watts, but with a rear-mounted drying fan and air flow circulation, food is dried evenly without rotating trays (Royaluxkitchen n.d.).

Cuisinart 5-Tray Food Dehydrator

This is a good dehydrator to get you started. It won't break the budget, and at 12 x 14 x 10.25 inches, it still gives you 552 square inches of drying space. The trays are transparent, BPA-free plastic, and come with an additional sheet for fruit leather. You can buy additional racks for stacking, and these are interlocking. The power rating is 620 watts, and there is a top venting system. The only downside is that the temperature settings are fan-only, low, medium, and high, so you don't have the same precision as other dehydrators (Cutler's n.d.).

Sahara Folding Dehydrator

This was one of the first dehydrators in the world that folds, saving you tons of space. In fact, you can have 11 feet of drying space in a dehydrator that folds to 22 x 12.25 x 3.75 inches. There are seven trays, and you can choose between stainless steel or polyplastic. Additional accessories include silicone drying mats and mesh drying sheets, but they are sold separately. You can set the time from 15 minutes to 99 hours. The temperatures range from 85°F to 165°F. With 700-watt dual heaters, you can begin with higher initial drying times, and then the dehydrator automatically switches to a lower temperature. The high efficiency of the circulating airflow, as well as the dual heaters and design, make this dehydrator more expensive (Brod & Taylor n.d.).

LEM Mighty Bite 5-Tray Countertop Dehydrator 1152

The Mighty Bite is a good mid-range dehydrator. The trays are 15 x 15 inches each, giving you 7.5 square feet of drying space. The trays are food-grade shatterproof ABS plastic with aluminum corners to reinforce them. There is a removable drip tray to make cleaning easier. On the top of the machine, there is a dial-knob for temperature settings from 95°F to 155°F in 10°F increments. The heating element is 500 watts, and the fan is rear-mounted. You can set the timer for up to 30 hours (Outdoor Home n.d.).

Elite Gourmet EFD319

This is the best budget option, but without any size specifications, you may not have the same drying capacity as others. There are five stackable, BPA-free trays that can be removed and placed in the dishwasher. You can choose between gray and transparent trays. Temperatures range from 95°F to 158°F. The power is 350 watts, but the machine dehydrates efficiently thanks to the base-mounted fan and horizontal airflow distribution (Elite Gourmet n.d.).

Sedona Express

At the other end of the scale, we have the Sedona Express with 11 trays, 9.9 square feet of drying space, and still only 12 x 19.6 x 14.5 inches. Aside from the 11 stainless steel trays, there is an extra stainless steel closed tray. With the LED digital display, you can set temperatures between 77°F and 167°F and times for up to 99 hours. There are a few features that justify the price tag. The first is the innovative settings with fast mode, raw mode (continuous temperatures of 118°F), and combo mode, which has different times and temperatures for different recipes. There is also the option to set higher initial temperatures and then have the dehydrator automatically switch to lower temperatures. What's more, you have a washable, reusable air filter, overheat protection, a non-flammable BPA-free plastic body, and a low wattage at just 470 watts (Tribest n.d.).

This brief guide to dehydrators and their features just goes to show how different machines can be and that it's not just the price you want to consider. Do you have the countertop space to keep one? Do you want materials that you can see through to check the process of your drying? Or is your main priority, a large drying surface, more important? Of course, a dehydrator isn't your only option, so for the rest of the chapter, we will consider other drying methods.

SUN DRYING VS. AIR DRYING

Both sun drying and air drying are ideal because they are free, but both require ideal conditions. For sun drying, you need temperatures of above 85°F and humidity levels of below 60 percent

(Nummer n.d.). A light breeze can also help speed up the drying process, which is usually a few days. As the air cools and condenses at night, moisture could be added back into the drying foods, so you will need to provide shelter overnight.

Not all foods are suitable for sun drying. Fruits are the best because of their high acid and sugar content. Vegetables are lower in both sugar and acid, so there is a greater risk of spoilage. Because meat is high in protein, sun drying can cause microbial growth. Meat should be treated with salt to inhibit microbial growth, but alternative methods are still safer.

You will need racks or screens to sun dry food. Much like a dehydrator, the material you choose is essential. Certain metals can leave harmful chemicals on your food. For example, copper destroys vitamin C. Stainless steel, food-grade plastic, or Teflon-coated fiberglass are all good options. You will also need a second rack to go on top to protect the food from birds and insects. Once you have chosen your racks, place them on blocks so they are slightly raised and get more air. It's also wise to place a sheet of metal under the blocks because the reflection of the sun can reduce drying times.

Air drying works on a similar principle, but high temperatures aren't required. Instead, moisture is removed from food by a warm breeze. The air is more important than the temperature. Foods are normally dried in smaller batches, and they are hung rather than placed on racks. You can dry fruits and mushrooms with this method, but I prefer it for my herbs. As the sun is not necessary, you can air dry food anywhere that has good ventilation, whether on your patio or in a room indoors.

OVEN DRYING VS. MICROWAVE DRYING

We have already covered the fact that oven drying is going to be more expensive than running a dehydrator, but that's not to say it isn't a viable option. Sometimes, I will use my oven to finish off food after being in the dehydrator, especially when I am doing bulk food drying. It's also a good option because you don't need to invest in any special equipment. Your oven should have come with racks, so you only need to line them with parchment paper. Sun drying and air drying are perfect for fruits and herbs, but the oven is a wonderful tool for fast, crispy vegetable snacks.

The main concern with the oven is the required temperature. We don't want to cook our food, and this is the purpose of an oven. Many ovens won't have low enough settings to actually remove the moisture. For this reason, you will likely need to leave the oven door slightly open. Even better, leave a fan close to the door for better circulation. The only equipment you might want to invest in is an oven thermometer to get a precise reading. Naturally, if you set your oven to a certain temperature and leave the door open, it won't be that simple to know how hot it is. That being said, if you have a convection oven, the chances are it can dehydrate food, too, so check your manual.

For oven drying, check your food more frequently, every hour or so. If your racks aren't fine enough to place food directly on them and you are using parchment paper, you may need to turn the food over for even drying.

You might not consider a microwave very practical for drying food, and it's true that you might be limited on space, but it's surprisingly efficient, with fruit slices being ready in as little as 30 minutes. Lay your ingredients on a microwavable dish, making sure they have enough space between them and set the timer for the recommended period. The one thing that you must remember is to use the defrost setting only. Fortunately, this mistake didn't cost me a lot of food, but my burned pear slices were something to laugh about, even after choosing a low setting.

CAN YOU DEHYDRATE FOOD IN AN AIR FRYER?

Air fryers have become increasingly popular over the last few years. It's only natural to want to get the most out of these kitchen gems. You can most definitely dry foods in an air fryer, but there are pros and cons. Like a microwave, you aren't going to have the same drying capacity as an oven or dehydrator. Because of the limited space for air circulation, it's necessary to provide enough space for your food with nothing overlapping.

The advantage of using an air fryer is the efficiency of these machines. They are excellent at circulating hot air evenly, so drying times are often shorter. This rapid air movement also helps lock in flavors. Most air fryers can be set to temperatures as low as 100°F. Because of their ability to remove moisture, be sure to keep an eye on your food to make sure you don't overly dry certain foods, especially things like jerky.

Dehydrating your food doesn't have to be done with just one method. Even with experience, I still love to experiment with different recipes and see how they turn out with different drying methods. Each method will have advantages and disadvantages depending on your desired outcome. Let's quickly summarize these!

Method	Pros	Cons
Dehydrator	Wide variety of features, excellent drying capacity, and cost-effective to run. Can be used for practically all food types.	Requires initial investment and may take up a lot of space.
Sun Drying	It's free, ideal for fruits, and doesn't require indoor space.	Conditions have to be right. Takes longer than other methods.
Air Drying	It's free, perfect for herbs, and can be achieved anywhere there is good ventilation.	Limited on types of food you can dry. Takes longer than other methods.
Oven Drying	No extra equipment is needed. Good for finishing off food when bulk drying. Ideal for vegetable snacks.	Can be expensive to run. Getting the right temperature is tricky.
Microwave Drying	No extra equipment is needed. It's faster than other methods.	Limited space.
Air Fryer	Excellent at even air circulation and heat distribution. Faster drying times than ovens and dehydrators. Good for enhanced flavor.	Limited space.

Hopefully, at this point, you will feel encouraged to use various methods to dry your food. What if you want to use a dehydrator but aren't in the position to buy one? Since catching the dehydration bug, I have become more aware of how much I waste. Now, I am determined to recycle and reuse more of what is lying around my home. Instead of purchasing a dehydrator, you are probably more than capable of making one and further reducing your carbon footprint. In the next chapter, it's time to get hands-on with a little DIY!

3

H—HOW TO MAKE YOUR OWN DEHYDRATOR

"Contentment is not about acquiring more, but being satisfied with greater simplicity and fulfilled by what you already have."

— CARLEY HAUCK

Not so long ago, we woke up to an unrecognizable world where suddenly, many of us were on strict lockdowns. Fortunately, the majority of us were able to jump online and order the necessary supplies. But what if this hadn't been an option? What if the next time a global disaster strikes, you had to make do with whatever you could find in your home? If you don't want to buy a dehydrator or you would rather upcycle materials you already have, making a dehydrator is a simple process. Let's begin with one design that requires minimal DIY skills.

A SIMPLE DEHYDRATOR FROM WINDOW SCREENS

What you will need:

- 2 Window screens
- 2 Hinges
- 1 Butt hinge catch lock or similar
- Food-grade sanitizer
- Round hooks (optional)

Instructions:

1. Sanitize the window screens. At this point, you may need to add a layer of cheesecloth if the mesh isn't thin enough to protect food from insects.
2. Attach the two hinges to one side of a window screen and then to the other.
3. On the opposite side of the window screens, attach the catch lock.
4. Additionally, you could add round hooks to one side of the screens so that you can hang the racks for better airflow.

The hinges and lock aren't necessary, but they are a nice extra. You can just place one screen on top of another, but for convenience and added protection from animals and the elements, I found this to be worthwhile. The last thing you want is a decent gust of wind blowing your racks over.

If you don't have window screens, you can make a basic frame with flat hardwood, screws, or strong wood glue. From there, you can staple a fine mesh to the frame, repeat this process for two frames, and join them the same way as you would the window screens. The beauty of the wooden frames is that you can customize the size to fit your needs.

THE TABLETOP DEHYDRATOR

What you will need:

- An old table
- 4 hardwood planks (the same length as the 4 sides of the table)
- Window screens (or DIY wooden frame screens as described above)
- Galvanized screws
- Scraps of hardwood
- A large sheet of glass or clear plastic
- 2 Hinges
- Acrylic glass adhesive
- Dark food-grade paint or varnish

Instructions:

1. Begin by drilling a row of large holes in the table approximately 8-10 inches apart. These will act as ventilation.
2. Attach the hardwood planks with galvanized screws to the outer edges of the table so you create a rim around the table.
3. Using the scraps of hardwood, measure and attach the pieces to the inside of the hardwood planks. These scraps will be the rims for the drying racks to sit on. If you are making your own racks, you can make them to the perfect size. If you are using window screens, you may

need to make them smaller or make larger rims for them to sit on.

4. Paint the tabletop, edges, and rims. The dark color will help absorb and maintain heat.

5. Cover the base of the table with fine wire mesh, or just cover the holes if you have scraps of mesh to use up, to prevent insects from getting inside the dehydrator.

6. Attach the hinges to one side of the table. Then, using acrylic glass adhesive, attach the other side of the hinges to the sheet of glass large enough to act as a lid for the dehydrator. The adhesive will also work on a sheet of plastic. It's important that your lid material is transparent to help trap heat from the sun.

This is a great way to upcycle a table, but you can also increase your drying space by choosing wider planks for the outer edges and adding inner rims for another layer of drying racks.

THE BOX DEHYDRATOR

This is a larger-scale dehydrator, but the size you choose will depend on how many shelves you want to add. As an example, I chose to make a box 19 x 16 inches because this was the ideal size to fit my old oven tray shelves. If you are using window screens, you can cut the plywood to the size of your screens. Or vice versa, if you are making your own racks, make them to the size of the plywood you have available.

What you will need:

- Sheets of plywood (½ inch or ¾ inch thick)
- Drying racks (window screens/oven trays/DIY racks)
- Wooden scraps
- Galvanized screws
- 3 100W light bulbs and sockets
- 2 Hinges (minimum)
- 1 Butt hinge catch lock or similar
- A small fan
- A thermometer
- Mesh scraps

Instructions:

1. Organize your plywood pieces so you know which are the sides, the top and base, and the back. Start by drilling ventilation holes in the top piece of plywood and down the piece of plywood that will be the back of your box. Cover the holes with fine mesh to prevent insects from entering.
2. Take the two sides of the box and lay them side by side. Measure the distance you want your racks to be (ideally around six inches apart). Leave extra space under the base of the last rack for your lights and fan. The amount of space will depend on the height of your fan, but I gave it an extra six inches of space between the fan and the bottom rack. Use wooden scraps as rims for the racks to sit on. Attach the scraps with galvanized screws.
3. If you have some extra wooden scraps, attach them to the plywood that will be the base of the box so that your dehydrator has legs and isn't sitting on the ground.

4. Using galvanized screws, attach the base and top to the back piece of plywood. Then, attach the sides, so that you have the structure of the box.

5. Take a final piece of plywood for the door. Attach the door using the hinges. If your box is quite tall, you may want to add a third hinge. Similarly, you may prefer to add another lock, too.

6. I have no electrical experience, so I bought a cheap lighting fixture that held three light bulbs and secured the fixture to the base of the box with small holes and wire. If you know what you are doing, you can buy separate lights and wire them together.

7. Place the fan on the floor of your box. You can also add a hook for your thermometer.

One day, I came across a sheet of glass that made a perfect fit for my door. So, I removed the door, cut a large hole in the plywood, and attached the glass with epoxy gel. Obviously, this made it easier to see the progress of the food without having to open the door and potentially adjust the temperatures.

THE UPCYCLED CABINET

What you will need:

- An old kitchen or bathroom cabinet
- Racks (same as before)
- Option 1: Lighting fixture, 100W light bulbs, fan
- Option 2: Dark food-grade paint or varnish

Instructions:

Really, this DIY dehydrator is a simplified version of the previous one, and you can choose your heating method depending on whether you want to use electricity or solar energy. The best thing is the structure of your box is already made. So, you just need to remove the current shelves and replace them with your racks.

I had one cupboard that had a wooden door, so it made sense to add the lights and fan. On the other hand, for the cupboard that had a large glass door, I just painted the inside and used solar energy to dry food. In both cases, I drilled ventilation holes and covered them with fine mesh.

TURNING YOUR OLD FRIDGE INTO A DEHYDRATOR

Please note that you can use the previously mentioned methods with a recycled fridge, but I'm going to give a couple of different options here that can also be used with other DIY dehydrators. It's all about the materials you have on hand.

What you will need:

- An old fridge
- A solar-powered light bulb
- A small solar-powered fan

Instructions:

1. If your fridge has a freezer compartment, you should remove it. Also, remove the shelving in the door by using a Stanley knife to break the sealant. You can fit an additional rack where the freezer compartment was.

2. When you remove the freezer compartment, you will notice a hole where the freezing tube was. You may need to make this hole bigger, but it's ideal for feeding the cables of the solar-powered fan and light bulbs.

3. Add a couple more large holes in the back of the fridge for ventilation. Again, you may need to cover these with fine mesh.

4. Place the fan and light bulbs on the bottom of the fridge and feed the cables through the hole. You may need to attach some fine mesh if the hole is large enough for insects to get in.

5. Place your dehydrator in a location that receives plenty of light. You might want to consider a backup battery to make sure you can store solar energy.

If you don't have the weather to rely on solar energy, replace the fan with a traditional electric fan, and instead of using light bulbs, repurpose the base of an old slow cooker or crock pot.

WHEN ALL YOU HAVE IS A CARDBOARD BOX AND A LAMP

I wouldn't say this is a long-term solution, but it is a fun DIY project, especially if you have children and you can start dehydrating today. This also isn't suitable for heavier foods because of the materials used.

What you will need:

- A sturdy cardboard box
- Extra sturdy card for racks
- A shoebox

- Lamp and lightbulb
- Duct tape
- Stanley knife or sharp cutting tool
- A twisty tie (like one you would find to close a loaf of bread)

Instructions:

1. Stand your box upright. Start with the extra study card and cut them into pieces that are slightly wider than your box but not longer. Cut spaces out of the middle of the pieces of the card to make shelves.
2. Along the sides of the box, cut slits evenly spaced apart so that your shelves can slot into the slits. Don't place the shelves in just yet.
3. In the base of the box, cut a hole large enough to fit the head of the lamp in. Use duct tape to secure the lamp in place.
4. Cut a space in the top of the shoebox so the lamp can sit inside and your cardboard box has a firm base. Cut a space in one end of the shoe box for the cable.
5. Slot the shelves into the spaces you made on the sides of the box. Use tape on the outside of the box to secure the shelves in place.
6. Poke holes in the sides and the bop of the box for ventilation. Use the twisty ties to keep the door closed.

Have a couple of lightbulbs of different wattages depending on the size of your cardboard box. Smaller boxes will need a lower wattage, so the heat doesn't end up cooking the food. You may also find that while your shelves don't last for too long, the structure of the dehydrator will so you can just replace the shelves when needed.

Granted, this isn't the most sophisticated dehydrator, but it just goes to show that you can dehydrate food with next to no equipment or materials and faster than air drying or sun drying.

There is one project on my to-do list for which I can't confirm the results just yet. For meats and certain other foods like nuts and definitely tomatoes, I love the idea of smoking and dehydrating at the same time. Hardwoods like oak can add a rich, smoky flavor to food, whereas maple wood can add a hint of sweetness to your dehydrated food.

My idea would be to use the tabletop design, but I wouldn't remove the base of the table. I plan to add the sides and the DIY racks, but instead of a glass top, I would use plastic, which will be easier to include a vent. On the underside of the table, I will have to cut a hole to fit the tubing that attaches the small wood burner to the dehydrator. I am excited to see (and taste) the results as well as discover how I can expand on my recipes and food prep.

Without sounding repetitive, I really want to take one last opportunity to emphasize flexibility and decision-making based on your goals. Most people will start dehydrating a few things at a time, so you may just need a couple of racks and experiment with your oven and air fryer. You may have the ideal kitchen cabinet that would provide you with tons of square feet for drying, but until you are ready to maximize that space, ask yourself if it's worth converting it into a dehydrator only to turn it on for a couple of shelves of food. You can even use a bit of outdoor space to store materials that will be useful for future DIY projects.

Don't overwhelm yourself trying to do it all at once. Imagine dehydrating your food like a new exercise regime. If you go all out at once, you risk giving up in the short run. There will always be time for dehydrating more food and filling up your pantry as long as the motivation remains!

You might be wondering why, at the end of another chapter, we still haven't covered the dehydration process. This is because the DEHYDRATE framework follows a logical process to avoid common mistakes. Now that you are aware of the dehydrating basics and the equipment you need, the next step is to jump into the dehydration process, get the most out of your yield, and reap even more benefits.

4

Y—YIELD OPTIMIZATION

"Preserve and treat food as you would your body, remembering that in time, food will be your body."

— B. W. RICHARDSON

Preserving your own food takes time, especially if you want enough in case of emergencies. But this is time incredibly well invested. We have seen all the benefits of dehydrated food. Now we get to appreciate that although food preparation and drying times require patience, the sky's the limit when it comes to filling your cupboard and body with nutritional and delicious food.

MAXIMIZING DRYING SPACE FOR FRUITS AND VEGETABLES

The first thing to keep in mind is that you want to choose fruits and vegetables that have similar drying times. It's senseless to put apricots in your dehydrator along with bananas, as the first takes around

30 hours and the second only 12 hours. The same can be said for temperatures. You want to be able to fill your dehydrator, turn it on, and leave it to save time and effort.

The preparation of fruits and vegetables is essential because you want to make sure there are no insects and bacteria. Running fruits and vegetables under cold water and gently scrubbing with a brush if necessary can help. For smaller fruits like berries, you can use a colander to rinse them.

Pretreatment of fruit is optional, but it can help retain color, texture, and nutrients, as well as increase shelf-life. For example, if you buy store-bought dried fruits, they will probably have been dipped in sulfur; that's why they have a bright color and reduce oxidation. Pretreatment is more recommended for light-colored fruits. Pretreating may also improve rehydration if you aren't just planning on fruit snacks.

To pretreat your food, you can use one cup of lemon juice added to four cups of water. Dip the fruit in the mixture for two minutes, but don't let it soak. Other juices can be added to water, but it's best to use those that are high in vitamin C, such as orange juice or pineapple juice.

Whether or not you peel your fruit is up to you. It's worth experimenting to discover the difference in textures and flavors. Nevertheless, blanching your fruit can be beneficial as it cracks the skin, which makes it easier for moisture to escape. For fruits like grapes, cherries, and blueberries that will be dehydrated whole, blanching is essential because if the skin isn't broken, moisture will remain. To blanch fruit, dip it in boiling water for 30-60 seconds and then dip it straight into ice-cold water. Blanching fruit like peaches and tomatoes for one or two minutes makes them easier to peel (Hodgens n.d.).

For dried vegetables, you will more likely look for a crispy texture, so steam blanching is a better option than hot water blanching. Steam blanching is still efficient at killing microorganisms and retaining nutrients, but it's a little gentler on the cell walls, so it may help vegetables keep their crunchy texture. Garlic, onions, leeks, and peppers don't need to be blanched before drying. To steam blanch vegetables, lay them in a basket that will allow steam to penetrate and place the basket on a pan of boiling water on the stove. Make sure the basket is three inches away from the boiling water (University of Minnesota Extension 2023). Be aware that steam blanching takes a few more minutes than blanching in hot water. There will be a more detailed guide on times further on.

Herbs are so forgiving and probably the easiest things to dry, regardless of the method you use. Begin by washing your herbs and gently patting them dry with kitchen paper; rubbing them dry can bruise the leaves. For sun drying or air drying, you can bunch herbs together and hang them to dry. It's important to hang your herbs upside down so all the active compounds and health benefits flow into the leaves. If you are using other methods, make sure the herbs are well spread on your trays for even drying. For sprigs like rosemary, it's easier to dry them on the stem, but for leafy herbs like basil, you will get better results if you spread leaves individually because they have a higher water content.

If you struggle to get your five a day, or you have children who are a little picky about their fruit and vegetables, leathers are great fun and an ideal way of hiding ingredients they would otherwise refuse. Making fruit and vegetable leathers requires cooking the necessary ingredients and turning them into a puree. If you are using light-colored fruit, it's worth adding two teaspoons of lemon juice for every two cups of fruit. Once you have your puree, pour it into a tray lined with a cookie sheet or nonstick foil until the layer is around ¼ inch thick. When the leather has been dehydrated and is still warm, peel the leather off the sheet, roll it up, and cut it into strips before allowing it to cool (LaBorde 2023).

In a perfect world, there would be just one list of drying times and temperatures, but if you have tried looking online for a simple answer, you probably haven't found one. There are too many influencing factors, such as your drying method, and even the same temperature can have different results depending on the brand of dehydrator. A good rule of thumb is to make sure herbs and vegetables are crisp and snap between your fingers. Successfully dried fruits will be pliable, and if you touch a dehydrated leather, it shouldn't leave any mark from your finger.

HOW TO GET THE MOST OF YOUR DRIED MEATS

I'm always up for a bit of experimentation with dehydrating food, but I have certain limits when it comes to meat because of the safety issues. Curing meat is one of the oldest methods of food preservation. The salt reduces the water available for bacteria to grow, but it doesn't take into consideration the possibility of larvae from worms that can be found in meat.

One particular concern is trichinella, a parasite that can be found in carnivorous animals. Eating even small amounts of raw or undercooked meat that has the larvae of this parasite may lead to trichinellosis, a rare disease that presents much like the flu. Freezing slices of pork at 5°F for 20 days can kill trichinella worms, but this is not effective for other meat from wild animals because the parasite may be freeze-resistant (CDC n.d.). I strongly urge you to cook all meat, poultry, and fish to the recommended temperature before dehydrating it.

Slicing meat is the best preparation for dehydration. Jerky is sliced and dehydrated meat, but once sliced, it's easy to cut into smaller pieces for meals or even grind the dehydrated meat into a powder. Attempting to dehydrate larger pieces of meat can lead to uneven drying and retained moisture that could encourage bacterial growth. It's also easier to cut slices when the meat is either partially defrosted or raw rather than attempting to cut even slices after cooking. When you are preparing the slices, cut away any fat that you can to ensure the meat is as lean as possible.

Despite wanting to remove moisture during the drying process, wet or moist heat is more effective in killing bacteria because the liquid penetrates tissues better. There are four ways you can pre-cook your meat slices prior to dehydrating:

- **Braising:** Seared in a hot pan and then cooked in a liquid (preferably in the oven) at a temperature of 275°F. This is better for tougher or older meat, and when you want the meat to absorb the flavors of the liquid.
- **Poaching:** Boiling in a liquid at temperatures of between 140°F and 180°F. The liquid at these temperatures should only bubble at the bottom of the pan, so it's ideal for cooking delicate food like fish.
- **Simmering:** The temperatures of liquids are between 180°F and 205°F. Food is cooked evenly in the liquid. It's a good option for meats you want to pull (like pulled pork) and dehydrate.
- **Boiling:** This is another good choice for tougher meats, and the higher temperature of at least 212°F makes it easier to break down tissues. As the bubbles are much stronger, avoid delicate foods when boiling (Alfaro 2019).

Use common sense when pre-cooking your meat. Of course, you want meat to absorb flavors and to be tender, but you also don't want your strips of meat to fall apart, especially not for jerky.

If you are drying ground meats, you will also need to pre-cook the meats. Don't forget to choose lean ground meat. Ground meats aren't always the best for rehydrating, so you might want to add some breadcrumbs to the meat beforehand. When rehydrating, the breadcrumbs allow more moisture to penetrate the dried meat, and the results are more tender. After pre-cooking, you can spread the ground meat on a tray or a rack with a sheet of cookie paper. A couple of times during the drying process, you will need to take a piece of kitchen paper and pat the excess moisture off the top.

Dehydration temperatures are important, but what you may have noticed is that when preparing meat, the pre-cooking temperatures are equally important. I strongly recommend investing in a digital cooking thermometer for accurate readings.

NUTS, GRAINS, AND OTHER HEALTHY SNACKS

For years, I would munch on nuts and seeds because they are often touted for their health benefits and nutritional value. I was convinced I was doing a good thing for my body until I learned about phytic acid. Phytic acid is an antioxidant, offering plenty of health benefits, but at the same time, it's also classed as an antinutrient. This is because it binds with different minerals in the meal you are eating, such as calcium, iron, manganese, and zinc. When this happens, the body can't absorb these nutrients (Valeii 2024). That's not to say foods containing phytic acid (nuts, seeds, grains, and legumes) should be avoided because the health benefits outweigh the downsides.

Soaking nuts and seeds in warm water and sea salt for between two and eight hours is ideal, but any soaking is better than none. Bigger nuts will benefit from longer soaking times. After soaking, pat the nuts and seeds dry with kitchen paper and then spread them on a tray or cookie sheet ready for the dehydrator. For grains and beans, cook them before dehydrating. Follow the instructions on the packet for cooking and then allow them to completely cool down before dehydrating them. Because you need to use trays or sheets for these small food parts, you may need to mix the tray content during the drying process so that the food dries evenly.

You might be wondering if it is worth dehydrating these types of foods, particularly when most come dried for a long shelf life anyway. For me, the biggest advantage of soaking or cooking these staple foods and then dehydrating them is the variety. Up to now, most of our drying has been connected with snacks, albeit amazing ones. We have crispy beet chips or fun nutritional leathers, but they aren't going to make a meal that ticks all your nutritional needs.

While dehydrated nuts and seeds can be a healthier snack, they can also be added to meals to make them more fulfilling. Once you master dehydrating things like lentils, grains, and beans, you have the ability to make hearty soups, stews, and even rice dishes like curries or a delicious stroganoff. Even things like bread and cakes can be sliced and placed on racks for dehydrating. When I dehydrated carrot cake, the slices became like cookies. They were crispy on the outside but still a little moist on the inside.

There is also the potential for greater savings. Commercial vendors are well aware of the rising trends in health foods (Naturis 2024) and prices are reflecting this. On top of that, for people with special dietary needs, dehydrating your own grains can reduce or even eliminate the need for far more expensive dietary alternatives. For example, someone who requires a gluten-free diet shouldn't have to pay more for gluten-free flour. Instead, almonds, oats, corn, and brown rice can all be dehydrated and ground into flour.

Don't worry if you aren't naturally inspired to jump into the kitchen and start making entire recipes with dehydrated foods. After we have looked at more techniques to enhance your dehydrating experience, we will discover some simple yet mouth-watering recipes.

TOP TIPS FOR CONSISTENT FOOD DRYING

For consistently good results, it's essential that your food slices are all the same thickness. If you have varying thicknesses, you will find that toward the end of the drying time, you will be picking out foods that are dry and leaving others for longer, which isn't the most productive use of your time.

A handy device is a mandolin. This piece of kitchen equipment often comes with various attachments, as well as the ability to adjust the thickness of the slices you want to create. The blades are incredibly sharp and can be used to slice meat, too. With a mandolin, you can slice, dice, and grate, and the results will always be uniform. With a mandolin, you can turn things like zucchini into zoodles (zucchini noodles) or sheets of zucchini for a lasagna alternative. You may even find a mandolin with a grinding plate for more options, such as ground spices, flour, and coffee beans. It's a kitchen gadget that I use for more than just preparing food for dehydration, so it's worth the investment.

How you position food on the trays can also impact your results. Food should definitely not overlap because this restricts the airflow, and you will end up with uneven results. Unless the instructions on your dehydrator state otherwise, you may find that you need to rotate the racks too.

Take care when dehydrating different foods together. It's best to dry members of the brassica family together and with no other food families in the dehydrator. Vegetables like cabbage, broccoli, cauliflower, and kale have sulfur-containing compounds that affect the flavor of other foods. Chilis can cause other foods to become a little spicier, although that can work to your advantage if you are drying them with something like tomatoes. I avoid putting foods with stronger flavors in a dehydrator or oven with other foods that have a mild flavor because of the potential transfer of flavors. This is especially true for onions. You know what onion vapor can do to your eyes; imagine the vapors when removing their moisture.

It's a good idea to step out of the mind frame that your dried food must look pretty and perfect. Choosing the best quality food is important. There is a difference between fruits and vegetables that are a little old and those that are a little bruised. The goal is to preserve as much food as possible, so imperfect fruits and vegetables are still ideal for dehydrating. Try to remember that if it tastes good it can be dehydrated regardless of its age. You may find that overripe food has more flavor, and it's a shame to throw this out because it doesn't look quite right. If you really don't like the look of something but the flavor is still there, use it to make leather.

The guide below will give you a better insight into drying times and temperatures, but it is only a guide. Don't be tempted to increase the temperature in an effort to reduce drying times. This often just leads to case hardening. Rapid drying causes sugars in a food to create a hard case around the food and seal moisture in, which only means food goes to waste.

To list every type of food for dehydrating would be impossible in this book but here is a good guide to get you started.

Fruits, Vegetables, and Herbs

Food Type	Temperature	Drying Times	Notes
Apples	135°F	10-12 hours	Core, slice, and pretreat
Bananas	130°F	9-11 hours	Peel, slice, and pretreat
Citrus Fruit	140°F	14-18 hours	Peel and slice
Grapes	135°F	18-22 hours	Blanch
Peach	135°F	12-16 hours	Halve, remove stone, and pretreat
Pineapple	140°F	10-14 hours	Peel, remove core, and slice
Tomatoes	135°F	8-10 hours	Blanch in hot water and slice or dice
Strawberries	130°F	8-10 hours	Halve or slice
Asparagus (medium stalks)	140°F	4-6 hours	Steam blanch for 5 minutes
Beans	125°F	6-8 hours	Steam blanch smaller beans for 3 minutes, and large beans for 6 minutes
Carrots	130°F	7-9 hours	Peel, dice, and steam blanch for 3 minutes
Corn	125°F	6-9 hours	Steam blanch for 6 minutes
Garlic	125°F	Up to 12 hours for cloves	Peel and slice or dice
Mushrooms	125°F	6-8 hours	Slice, pretreat, and steam blanch for 5 minutes
Onions	135°F	8-10 hours	Peel and cut into rings or dice

Peas	125°F	5-7 hours	Steam blanch for 3-5 minutes
Peppers	125°F	6-8 hours	Cut into rings or slices
Potatoes	135°F	6-8 hours	Dice, slice, or shred and steam blanch for 4-5 minutes
Squash	130°F	8-10 hours	Peel, slice, and steam blanche for 4-5 minutes
Turnips/Parsnips	125°F	10-12 hours	Peel, slice, and steam blanch for 5 minutes
Zucchini	135°F	8-9 hours	Slice and steam blanch for 1-2 minutes
Herbs	100°F	1-4 hours	Spread individual leaves or dry sprigs whole

Meat, Fish, and Poultry

Food Type	Temperature	Time	Notes
Beef	165°F	4-5 hours	Precook to 160°F
Lamb			
Chicken	145°F	6-8 hours	Precook to 165°F
Turkey	140°F	6-8 hours	Precook to 165°F
Fish	145°F	12-14 hours	Precook to 145°F
Rabbit	145°F	8-12 hours	Precook to 160°F
Venison	140°F	8-10 hours	Precook to 165°F
Ground meats	145°F	6-8 hours	Precook to 160°F

Nuts, Seeds, Grains, and Beans

Food Type	Temperature	Drying Times	Notes
Almonds	155°F	10-12 hours	Soak for 8-12 hours
Brazil	150°F	12-15 hours	Soak for 8 hours
Cashew	145°F	4-6 hours	Soak for 4 hours
Hazelnut	105°F	Minimum 8 hours	Soak for 8 hours
Pecan	115°F	6-9 hours	Soak for 6 hours
Sunflower seeds	105°F	4-6 hours	Soak for 4 hours
Pumpkin seeds	115°F	1-2 hours	Soal for 4 hours
Pine nuts	115°F	3-4 hours	Soak for 4 hours
Rice	125°F	5 hours	Precook according to instructions
Pasta	135°F	2-4 hours	Precook according to instructions
Lentils	125°F	10 hours	Precook according to instructions
Chickpeas	125°F	8-12 hours	Precook according to instructions

Nothing is set in stone. For example, if you want to bulk dry some of your staples, you can add rice, pasta, lentils, and chickpeas to the dehydrator at a temperature of 125°F, removing the rice tray after five hours and expecting the pasta to take a little longer than it would at 135°F.

It's taken a lot of trial and error to get these guidelines, and I have to emphasize again the varying factors. I kept a journal where I could record exactly how I had pretreated foods, the temperatures I set, the time they were dehydrated, and the results (referring to the flavor and texture). With these notes, it was easier to make small tweaks and get the perfect results I was aiming for.

On the one hand, there are drying techniques such as air, oven, or dehydrator. On the other hand, there are culinary techniques that can improve the dehydrating experience as well as the flavor of food. We will delve into these culinary techniques in the next chapter.

5

D—DRYING FOR THE LONG TERM

"The food you eat can either be the safest and most powerful form of medicine or the slowest form of poison."

— ANN WIGMORE

We have already seen how the Western diet isn't exactly helping us, and although poison sounds like a strong word, over time, a diet that isn't balanced can have horrendous consequences. In this chapter, we are going to make sure our dehydrated food isn't just better for us but retains the most nutrients and adds to the health benefits. One of the essential parts of drying food is to make sure they are stored safely so that your cupboards are stocked for months, if not years.

EXACTLY HOW LONG CAN DEHYDRATED FOOD LAST?

Let's say the peaches that you bought are now four days old and you spend multiple hours drying them only to make a mistake with storage and have to throw out the entire batch. Knowing how to store your dehydrated food is what is going to make your efforts worthwhile. It's what is going to make a fresh peach last for up to a year instead of just days.

There are several factors that will influence the shelf life of your food, including moisture, oxygen, temperature, light, and pests. Foods prior to being hydrated are at greater risk of microbial growth and mold, so it makes sense that any moisture in your stored dried food can encourage bacteria growth, resulting in not just a shorter shelf life but also spoilage. Too much oxygen can have similar consequences. Food can spoil more quickly when exposed to too much oxygen because the process of oxidation occurs, and microorganisms start to grow, leading to mold and yeast growth. Oxidation may also cause food to go brown and smell awful because chemical reactions happen at a faster rate. Unfortunately, high temperatures can also speed up the growth of bacteria and mold.

Another process to watch out for is photodegradation because of too much natural or artificial light. This can lead to a loss of color and flavor, but what's worse is that food could start to lose its nutritional value (Valley Food Storage 2023). Insects and other pests are going to love your dehydrated food as much as you do. I'm convinced that as soon as one problem pest arrives, they tell their friends about their new food source, and before you know it, you will have an entire infestation ready to spoil more than just your dehydrated food.

With the right conditions and storage techniques, which will be discussed in a bit, most of your dried food will last for around a year, but it's interesting to know that the shelf-life might even be a lot longer. Excalibur is one of the leading brands in food dehydrators and below you can find the company's average shelf life of certain foods.

Food Type	Average Shelf Life After Dehydration
Apples	20-25 years
Baker's Flour	12-15 years
Broccoli	8-10 years
Cheese Powder	10-15 years
Corn	8-12 years
Fruit (most)	3-5 years
Granola	4-5 years
Honey, Salt, Sugar	Indefinitely
Kidney Beans	18-20 years
Onions	8-12 years
Peppers	8-12 years
Potatoes	20-30 years
Powder Eggs/Milk	15-20 years
Spaghetti	15-20 years
White Rice	8-10 years

(Excalibur 2014)

You might question the indefinite shelf life of honey, but raw honey has amazing antibacterial properties which keep it safe, and it also has the natural ability to maintain flavor and nutrients. In 2012, archeologists found jars of edible wildflower honey in Egyptian tombs that were 5,000 years old (Colangelo 2023).

Fortunately, I'm not old enough to have 25-year-old dehydrated apple slices to confirm the shelf life. In a realistic world, I can't imagine needing to dehydrate more than two decades of any fruit. However, with the correct preparation and storage, you can now see that with care, there is a practical way to keep your cupboards or pantry well stocked with a variety of food for an emergency.

The question that burned in my mind was why some people say dehydrated food can last for up to a year, and others state it is so much longer. This comes down to the importance of storing your food the right way.

THE BENEFITS OF VACUUMING DRIED FOOD

Once you have made your favorite jerky recipe, the meat will be good for up to two months, which is still far longer than simply keeping it in your fridge. Professionally dehydrated meats can last for up to 10 years (Laliberte 2022), and longer if kept in the freezer. This huge difference is because the dehydrated meat has been vacuum sealed.

Dehydration removes the moisture from food but the moment you vacuum seal food, you are also removing the oxygen and preventing spoilage from bacteria and other microorganisms. Without air coming into contact with your food, aside from the safety aspect, you can also maintain the flavor and texture of dehydrated food. Generally speaking, food that is vacuum-sealed lasts five times longer than other sealing methods, and that's before considering the longer shelf life after dehydration (Vacpac 2023).

Vacuum sealing your food goes beyond extending the shelf life while maintaining nutritional value. Removing the air from products significantly reduces the amount of space items take up, giving you even more room for your delicious ingredients. It's also another way to increase your savings. Let's say you don't have time to prepare and dehydrate food, or there are offers on in your local store, and you won't get around to drying it all. Using a vacuum sealer gives you some additional leeway with your time. Vacuum sealing before dehydrating retains moisture and flavor, so you don't need to worry about reduced quality of food.

The process of vacuuming your food is simple. Many vacuum sealers come with a few sample bags; however, it's often best to invest in a roll of vacuum sealing bag that can be cut to the ideal size for your food. Bags are made of plastic and non-reusable, so you want to try to reduce as much waste as possible. If you are looking to buy a vacuum sealer, try to find one with a built-in bag cutter for convenience.

Once you have cut your bag to the ideal size, seal one end. Most machines are automatic and will stop when the bag end is sealed, though you may want to play it safe and double seal the ends. Food should always be completely cooled before vacuum sealing. Because dehydrated food is often quite sharp, it makes sense to wrap food in a cookie sheet and then place it in the bag. This will help prevent the sharper edges of food from piercing the bag and letting oxygen in. When you are filling your bags, aim for portion sizes or, at the very least, the amount of food that you will use at a certain time. If you are dehydrating and vacuum sealing entire meals, it's sensible to pack individual portions or portions for two people. After filling your bags, you can seal the other end and store them.

Another handy addition that comes with some vacuum sealers is a jar sealing kit that allows you to use mason jars with special lids to vacuum seal contents in jars. The advantage of jars is that the lids are reusable. The downside is that you aren't saving as much space as you do with bags. For this reason, I use both options. For freezing food, I use bags because I can get more in smaller spaces, but for many of my dried goods in the pantry, I prefer jars. On a non-dehydrating note, but still related to food preservation, you can also find a vacuum-sealing accessory for bottles that can extend the shelf life of wines, oils, and bottles of vinegar.

The cost of a vacuum sealer depends on the quality and accessories that come with it, but, like my mandolin, it's a piece of kitchen equipment that has proven to be invaluable for food preservation.

STORAGE SOLUTIONS AND BONUS PANTRY ORGANIZATION TIPS

Drying, vacuuming, and freezing foods is a process that is going to allow for the longest possible shelf life but there are other options because I know my freezer isn't large enough to hold everything and, sometimes, I want dried ingredients ready to use without defrosting.

As we discussed before, storage locations need to have the ideal conditions for long-term storage. The area needs to be dark, cool, and dry. Temperatures should be 60°F or lower, so while a fridge can also be used for longer storage times (with ideal fridges set at a temperature of 40°F), it's not necessary to store all your dried goods here (Huffstetler 2023). If you are planning to keep foods on the kitchen sides, which is common for items that are used regularly, like herbs and spices, it's best to keep smaller jars and have a larger supply in a cooler, darker location as they will deteriorate faster with the conditions of the kitchen. If you start to run out of shelf space, consider upcycling an old chest of drawers.

If you aren't ready to invest in a vacuum sealer, there is an alternative that will remove oxygen to store food for longer, but it won't be as effective as vacuum sealing. Oxygen absorbers can be bought in bulk and added to jars. Although they aren't reusable, you can use every day mason jars without any special equipment. Be sure to fill the jars as much as possible because this leaves less room for oxygen and the absorbers can be more effective.

Oxygen absorbers come in different capacities. For example, 50cc (cubic centimeters) is ideal for half-pint jars, but 100cc is better for pint jars. For larger jars, you can find 100cc oxygen absorbers, or you may want to use two or three of the smaller ones (Backpacking Chef n.d.). Sealable bags can be used with oxygen absorbers, but we go back to the issue of using plastic unnecessarily. If you choose sealable bags, they will have to be ones that can be heat sealed so that they are effective.

Regardless of whether you store your dried food in jars, plastic bags, in the fridge, freezer, or pantry, there is one thing you should get into the habit of doing from day one. Even if you have only just air dried your first batch of herbs, label your storage choice with the items and the date that you prepared them. I know you will tell yourself you will remember what they are, but after a couple of weekends with your dehydrating methods, you will start to collect an impressive number of different ingredients, and you only need a few stressful weeks and a full brain to forget what is what.

Correctly labeling your food also makes it easier to stick to the "first in and first out" storage method. It's a regrettable mistake that I made, and you may have done the same with other foods. When you come home from shopping, an already dreaded task of mine, you still need to put everything away. Typically, you just put things in the first space you can find, pushing older produce to the back. If you don't do this, I commend your patience! When it comes to a good clear-out, there are tins and packets of food that are well past their best-by date. While starting the new habit of labeling everything, be strict about putting your freshly dehydrated goods behind those you have previously prepared. It's a good practice for your fridge and freezer, as well as cupboards and pantry shelves.

HOW TO REHYDRATE FOOD

So much emphasis is placed on dehydrating food but there is very little information on rehydrating. Yes, it's a pretty simple process but it doesn't mean there aren't tips to ensure you are getting the most out of everything you rehydrate. Of course, how you rehydrate your food will depend on the intended purpose. Before looking at specifics, let's cover the basics.

The most basic way to rehydrate food is to place the contents in a bowl and add water. You should add enough to cover the contents and then an inch or two extra. Don't worry if all the extra water isn't absorbed because it won't go to waste. Any excess water can be used for cooking. Leave the contents to soak overnight, and the next morning, you will have ingredients ready to cook with. To speed this up, you can start soaking in hot water rather than cold water, but you will still be looking at several hours for rehydration.

A second option is to simmer your dried food. Again, you will need enough water to cover the contents and a little extra. When started in hot water, generally, dried food will take approximately 10 minutes of simmering to rehydrate, but you can also turn the heat off and leave the ingredients for longer in the hot water to finish.

Remember, rehydrating through simmering isn't the same as cooking food. This is less relevant for meats because they will have been precooked, as well as for other precooked foods prior to dehydrating, such as pasta, rice, and grains. It's also less relevant if you are using ingredients to add during the cooking process. For example, if you are adding dehydrated vegetables to a stew, the cooking time and correct amount of fluids will ensure that they are both rehydrated and cooked.

The good thing about rehydrating food is that it's not an exact science and there is always room for adding more water if needed.

Fish is the exception when it comes to rehydration. Because of the changes in cell structure during cooking, it's harder to rehydrate fish to get the same texture as you would expect from freshly cooked. To overcome this problem, I have found that soaking fish in saltwater for 24 hours and then soaking it in milk for another hour or two helps. The milk sounds bizarre, but it helps remove the overly salty flavor from the salt water. If you are making a recipe that results in a creamy sauce, you could also poach the fish in milk.

Now for the fun side of rehydrating. Once you have experimented with water for rehydration, there is nothing stopping you from using other liquids. Rehydrating meat and vegetables with stock can enhance flavors. I am a big fan of curries, and for that reason, I use coconut water to rehydrate meat and chicken. Fruits can be paired with juices for interesting combinations, and you would be surprised by the tastiness of fruit that is rehydrated in different teas. Depending on who you are cooking for, you may also want to rehydrate your food with alcohol. The chances of getting intoxicated from your food are very slim, but even after an hour of cooking, 25 percent of the alcohol can be retained (London 2023).

One final point about rehydrating—I would use your journal to keep notes about the rehydration method you use (time and liquid choice, too) so that you can narrow down the ultimate techniques for your taste buds.

MAKING MEALS WITH DEHYDRATED FOODS

We are going to use an example of a tuna pasta bake to cover two methods for making an entire meal. Although you can switch any of the ingredients, I tend to use elbow macaroni because it rehydrates better. Then, I use carrots, onions, peas, and tuna. Honestly, frozen peas work just as well. It's only logical that you haven't mastered dehydrating and rehydrating tuna yet, so for convenience, you can use store-bought canned tuna.

The first method would be to cook the pasta (al dente), peel and dice the carrots and partially cook them, and peel and dice the onions and gently sauté them until partially cooked. As you are cooking these ingredients, you can add any herbs and spices you feel will pair well. Leave all the parts to cool before dehydrating them. You can then mix the three dried ingredients and seal them in an airtight jar for when you are ready to use them. To construct the meal, you can add stock to the dehydrated ingredients, then add the peas and tuna, and simmer for 5-10 minutes until you have the texture you want. If you didn't add herbs, spices, salt, and pepper during the cooking process, now is a good time to make any final tweaks.

The alternative method is to cook the pasta the same way you normally would. In my case, I sauté the onions, add the diced carrots, pasta, stock, herbs, and spices, and cook for half the recommended time the pasta needs. At the last minute, I add peas and tuna. Remember, you don't want to cook the food fully because when simmering, the ingredients will both rehydrate and finish cooking. Once the meal has completely cooled, you can spread the ingredients on a cookie sheet and dehydrate the entire meal. Don't add any excess stock to the sheet because it will only increase the drying time.

The second method is easier on the one hand, but also trickier because different ingredients have different dehydration times. I make sure that those foods with longer drying times are cut into smaller pieces to help balance the process out. While you are starting out, you might want to try combining the two methods, dehydrate those foods that require more time separately, and add them to the main meal when simmering. The options are limitless!

Test Your Skills

Let's make a hearty, fully dehydrated meal of slow-cooked beef and mushrooms with mashed potatoes. I won't tell you the whole process because you have all the techniques you need. My tip would be to sauté the beef before slow cooking with the mushrooms in a beef stock. Mashed potatoes can be dehydrated at a temperature of 135°F for 8-10 hours until it is brittle. If you are feeling adventurous, reduce the stock and pour it onto a tray with slightly raised edges. You can dehydrate the stock at the same time as the mashed potatoes and then grind it into a powder. Rehydrating this powder will give you the perfect gravy to go with your beef and mash.

If you don't have all the ingredients to make the suggested meal above, don't worry. I can almost guarantee you have something in your fridge or in your cupboards that will benefit from being dehydrated. Don't put it off or think that now isn't the right time. Don't fear making a mistake. Take those first small steps so you are ready for the next chapter. You aren't going to buy, let alone make a dehydrator just for a few dried fruit and vegetable snacks. Now is the time to explore more dehydrated recipes that tick the nutritious and delicious boxes.

YOU DON'T NEED STRICT OR BORING DIETS TO TAKE CARE OF YOUR WELL-BEING—TODAY AND FOR THE FUTURE

"Stop eating 'dead' food: junk, fried, and fast foods, as well as processed carbs. They are loaded with sugar and other additives. The more live foods we eat (fruits and vegetables), the more alive we feel. The more dead foods we eat…well, you get the idea."

— TONY HORTON

We have heard time and time again that we are what we eat, but it's not easy making the necessary changes. Processed foods are quick and easy, and with hectic lifestyles this is often all we have time to cook. But over time, this is going to have significant consequences.

As we reach this point, you are fully aware of the nutritional value of dehydrated foods and the practicalities of having a well-stocked pantry, fridge, and freezer. There is immense peace of mind when you know you have enough delicious and healthy food that will last you for more than a year.

The problem is, and you may have found this to be true for yourself in the past, that when people think of dehydrated food, their minds head straight to jerky. Would you really go to all that effort of getting a dehydrator for a few bits of dried meat without the reassurance that it's tasty, let alone safe?

Unfortunately, with this idea of dehydrated foods, people are often put off and this means they are stuck relying on unhealthy options, resulting in poor health. This may only be exacerbated in times of emergency.

You don't have to be a dehydration master to help these people see just how much can be achieved when drying your own food, even if they don't have a dehydrator. People need to hear real experiences from readers just like you.

When you share your opinions of this book on Amazon, others get to see that they too can dehydrate a wide range of foods without expensive equipment or specialist skills. They too can improve their health while leading more sustainable lives.

I know you are super busy, and you would probably rather be in the kitchen preparing food, so I promise the process is simple and only takes a few minutes. Reviews are also the perfect way to share ideas and inspiration. I can't wait to hear what you have been up to with your food. Speaking of inspiration, it's time to explore some recipes!

Scan the QR code below:

6

R—RECIPES AND APPLICATIONS

> *"Just because food is served fast doesn't mean it has to be made with cheap raw ingredients, highly processed with preservatives and fillers and stabilizers and artificial colors and flavors."*
>
> — STEVE ELLIS

Fast food is synonymous with restaurants that have poor-quality ingredients that have been highly processed, packed with preservatives, and seasoned with goodness knows what else to provide some form of flavor. But as Ellis states, this doesn't have to be the case.

I put this to the test, and I found that, very generally speaking, you can expect to wait for around five minutes for a meal in a fast-food restaurant. While the time isn't bad, we have to question the quality and the price. Let's estimate the average price of a fast-food meal at $10. For the same price as the meal for a family of four, I know I can get various vegetables, rice, pasta, and chicken, which can easily make more than four meals. From experience, I know that if I soak my ingredients overnight to rehydrate them, I can heat up a nutritious and fulfilling soup in around five minutes. It's a no-brainer!

Despite your dehydrated food needing more preparation, once your cupboards and freezer start to fill up, you can imagine your own little fast-food restaurant at home, one that surpasses anything you can experience out and about, at least in my humble opinion. To achieve this, you might need some inspiration to get you started.

With the recipes below, I haven't included specific quantities because I always feel that people should adjust the amounts of ingredients depending on their own taste buds. I also find that, sometimes, we come across recipes that we are keen to try, but we are missing one ingredient, and that's enough to put us off. Please, feel free to change any ingredient that you don't like or don't have to something that you would prefer. On a similar note, spice them up any way you fancy. I'm not going to add salt and pepper to each of the savory recipes, but both are highly recommended.

One final note—you will notice that there is some sautéing in the preparation of the main meals. Try to use the least amount of butter or oil because, if you remember, fats do not dehydrate well.

SNACKS AND SIDES

Hash Browns

Ingredients

- Potatoes
- Onion
- Lemon juice

Steps

Peel and shred the potatoes. Place the shredded potatoes straight into cold water because if not, oxygen will turn them brown quickly. Drain the water and add fresh water with lemon juice. Leave the potatoes in the water while you peel and shred the onions. Avoid shredding the root end of the onion because this is the part that may make you cry more.

Drain the shredded potatoes again and then add them to boiling water to blanch them. While they are blanching, squeeze any excess juice from the shredded onion and sauté it until it is soft. Remove the shredded potatoes once they are fork-tender, and leave them and the onion to cool. It's best to leave the potatoes in a colander so excess liquid can drain off. You may also need to pat the potatoes with a kitchen towel if they still feel moist.

Spread the potatoes and onion on trays. Shredded potatoes and onion will need a temperature of 135°F for 8-10 hours, meaning you can mix the two ingredients or dehydrate them on separate trays. To rehydrate, add your desired amounts of shredded potatoes and onion to a bowl and leave to soak for around 15 minutes. Then drain, squeeze off any excess liquid, add your spices, shape them, and fry them.

Salt & Vinegar Cucumber and Kale Chips

Ingredients

- Kale
- Cucumber
- Olive oil
- Salt
- Vinegar

Steps

Begin by removing all the kale leaves from their stems. Stems, once dehydrated, can end up like sticks, but don't waste them. You can add the stems to stocks for more flavor. Blanch the kale leaves for around three minutes.

Slice the cucumber and blanch it for about two minutes. This will help remove the waxy coating.

Kale and cucumber require different drying times, so it's best to keep the ingredients separate, but the initial preparation is the same. After blanching, leave the food to cool. Then, toss with olive oil, vinegar, and salt.

Spread the kale and cucumber on different trays. The kale chips will take around eight hours at 110°F, and the cucumber needs around the same time, possibly up to 10 hours at 130°F. You can eat them separately, but I like the combination of the flavors, so I mix the dried ingredients together.

Trail Mix

Ingredients

- Apples
- Bananas
- Mango
- Cranberries
- Grapes
- Coconut
- Nuts of your choice (almonds, cashews, hazelnuts, pistachios)
- Sunflower seeds
- Pumpkin seeds
- Ginger

Steps

Don't feel you need to add all the ingredients. This type of recipe is often best for things you already have prepared. Just grab a handful of each to make a healthy snack. We have seen how to use lemon and blanching for fruit, and how to soak nuts and seeds before dehydrating. The only additional information we need is for the coconut and ginger.

Prepare your coconut the same way you normally would by using a screwdriver to find the soft eye and make a hole to drain the liquid. Tap along the seam to crack the coconut and remove the outer shell and inner husk. Blanching coconut for five minutes can help preserve the color. If you want slices, aim for around ¼ inch thick and dehydrate at 130°F for 8-10 hours. Shredded coconut can be dehydrated at 105°F for 6-8 hours. Shorter drying times will lead to a chewy texture, and longer drying times will allow for crunchy coconut.

Ginger can be peeled, but it's not always necessary. If the skin is quite rough and woody, you are better off peeling it. There are different preparation methods, such as grating, shredding, or slicing. Once you have prepared the ginger, lay it out on trays or sheets if grated or shredded. I prefer using lower temperatures, around 95°F, because you end up with a better flavor, and it still only takes around 4-6 hours to dry. You will know when it's properly dried because it will snap when you break it.

Tomato Soup

Ingredients

- Tomatoes
- Onion
- Celery
- Butter or olive oil
- Herbs of your choice
- 1 tsp sugar
- Cream
- Stock

Ingredients

If using fresh tomatoes, blanch them to make peeling easier, and then cut them into slices. Peel and chop the onion. Chop the celery. With a little butter or olive oil, sauté the onions and celery. When soft, add the tomatoes, sugar, and herbs of your choice. Add the stock and cream to get the consistency you like. Then, either use a food processor or an immersion (stick) blender to make a smooth, creamy soup.

When the soup has cooled, spread it evenly onto trays. It will take about 8-12 hours to dehydrate the soup at a temperature of 135°F. You will know when it's fully dry because it won't be sticky to the touch.

You can break the dehydrated soup into smaller pieces or grind it into a powder. To rehydrate your soup, add the right amount of water or stock and simmer until hot. You can always add more water/stock during the cooking process.

Mushroom Pesto

Ingredients

- Mushrooms (button, cremini, oyster, portobello)
- Spinach
- Shallots
- Walnuts
- Garlic
- Pinenuts
- Parmesan
- Olive oil

Steps

This is a bonus recipe because you have two recipes in one. The first is to combine all of your ingredients in a blender to make the pesto. It should be coarsely chopped rather than a smooth paste. Spread the pesto onto a cookie sheet and dehydrate at 120°F for 6-7 hours until it is brittle. Rehydrate using the cold soaking method, adding more water after a few hours if need be. You can add this pesto to toast, use it as a dip for your vegetable chips, or add it to pasta.

An alternative is to leave the mushrooms whole and blend all of the other ingredients to the right consistency. Remove the stems from the mushrooms and spoon the pesto into the caps of the mushrooms. Place them on a rack and dehydrate them at 100°F for 5-6 hours for bite-sized snacks.

MAIN MEALS

Risotto

Ingredients (Traditional)

- Shallots or onion
- Garlic
- Rice
- Mascarpone
- Sharp cheddar
- White wine (optional but better)
- Stock

Possible Alternative Ingredients

- Peas
- Red Bell Peppers
- Asparagus
- Ricotta
- Mushrooms

Method

For risotto, I like to have the base of the meal prepared and dehydrated. When it comes to the alternative ingredients, I mix them in before rehydrating. This way, I can use up the ingredients I have, and it's not always the same risotto. The exception would be the ricotta, which I add towards the end of cooking.

Begin by peeling and chopping the shallots (or onion) and sautéing them until almost soft. Peel and dice the garlic, add it to the shallots, and leave for a couple of minutes. Add the rice and a decent splash of wine and mix well. Turn the heat down and gradually add the stock until the rice is cooked. Finally, add the mascarpone and sharp cheddar, as well as any seasoning to taste.

Leave the risotto to completely cool before spreading it on a cookie sheet or tray. Making sure the rice is evenly spread will help with a consistent finish. This can be helped by turning the rice over halfway during the drying time, which can be from 4-8 hours at 135°F.

From here, you can either store the brittle dehydrated rice or add other dried ingredients and store them as ready-prepared meals.

Vegetable Stew

Ingredients

- Potatoes
- Onion
- Celery
- Carrot
- Parsnips
- Stock (beef or vegetable)
- Dehydrated tomato soup

Method

The trick to the most amazing, rehydrated stew is all in the preparation of your vegetables. You can cook (add all the prepared ingredients and slow cook) your stew and dehydrate it in the same way as your risotto. It's best to separate the liquid from the vegetables and dehydrate them separately. The dehydrated liquid and vegetables can be mixed together for rehydration and cooking.

On the other hand, you can choose the dehydrated vegetables that you have already prepared. However, you will probably notice that if you just add stock to your vegetables, you will end up with quite a liquid stew rather than the hearty stew you might be expecting. This is where the dehydrated tomato soup helps. Adding some can improve the flavor and consistency of the stew.

Another favorite of mine for stews is to make vegetable leathers. Much like mashed potatoes, you can pre-cook root vegetables, mash them, and dehydrate them. Once they are dehydrated, you can break them into pieces or grind them into a powder. These vegetable leathers are ideal for thickening up stews and other meals, as well as for a nutritious snack.

When rehydrating food for stews, it's all about timing. Consider the size of your vegetables because potatoes are going to require more time than, say, peas. I have found it's easier to start simmering the larger ingredients along with the vegetable leathers and dehydrated soup and adding smaller vegetables. This way, all of your vegetables are cooked properly, and the flavors of the stock and tomato have time to infuse.

Paella

Ingredients

- Bell peppers
- Onion
- Garlic

- Shrimp
- Crab meat
- Chicken
- Short grain rice
- Chicken/fish stock
- Paprika
- Saffron
- White wine (optional but better)

Possible alternative/additional ingredients

- Rabbit
- Tomato
- Spanish chorizo
- Mussels

Method

Paella comes in such a range of varieties when it comes to ingredients, but, typically, it's a combination of seafood and chicken or rabbit. For dehydrated paella, I use shrimp and crab meat because they tend to rehydrate better. For the basics, begin by sautéing the onion and garlic. Add the diced peppers and then the chicken. Add a generous splash of wine. Leave to simmer for 5 minutes. Add the rice, stock, paprika, and saffron, and cook as per the instructions on the packet. Remember that you can dry your own red peppers and grind them into a powder to make paprika. Once cooled, spread the paella on trays and dehydrate for 8-10 hours at 140°F.

There will come a point where your cupboards are well stocked with different ingredients, and you may prefer a different method. For example, I often have chicken and tomatoes ready in jars, so I would add these in during rehydration. Even the bell peppers, shrimp, and crab meat can be added later. The most important things to add when cooking the rice are the wine, stock, paprika, and saffron because this is what gives the rice the typical color (and flavor) of paella.

A word of warning when it comes to using chorizo. This meat adds a wonderful depth to paella, but it is high in fat. It's common to fry the chorizo and remove it from the pan before sautéing the onions for added flavor, but I wouldn't recommend this for dehydrating. Instead, if you want to add chorizo, try frying it and add it when the paella is cooking. Mussels are one of the most iconic parts of Spanish paella, but I also wouldn't start dehydrating them as they are best fresh. Instead, 5 minutes before the paella is ready, place the mussels on the rice and cover, taking care that the rice doesn't dry out. When the mussels open, they are cooked.

Chili Mac

Ingredients

- Elbow pasta or similar
- Lean ground beef
- Breadcrumbs
- Onion
- Kidney beans
- Tomatoes
- Chili powder
- Paprika
- Dried oregano
- Cheddar

Method

There are two ways to make chili mac. You can make the sauce and the pasta and dehydrate them together, or you can make the sauce and dehydrate it separately. For camping or day trips, I prepare it together, but in my long-term storage, I have just the sauce because sometimes I will make it with pasta and other times with rice. A separate sauce is handy if you don't have elbow pasta (or similar) because it is best for storage. Also, if you have the ingredients dehydrated separately, you can combine them and then rehydrate and cook them.

The sauce is simple to make. Remember to mix breadcrumbs into the ground beef, even if you are going to use it in a sauce. It will make all the difference when rehydrating. Sauté your onions and add the ground beef. When the meat is brown, you may want to pat any excess fat with kitchen paper, taking care not to burn yourself. Then, add all of the other ingredients except the cheese. Don't forget that if you don't want to use whole or canned tomatoes, you can use your dehydrated tomato soup, which will help thicken your chili. You can make your own chili powder by dehydrating chilies and grinding them into a powder. Dehydrate your chili at 145°F for 6-8 hours.

The reason you don't want to add cheese to the sauce is because of the fat content. For peace of mind, I dehydrate cheese separately and grind it into a powder. This cheese powder can be used for dozens of other recipes, from biscuits to sauces and salads. Preparation will depend on the type of cheese. Hard cheese needs to be grated, whereas softer cheeses, like feta, need to have as much moisture removed beforehand. The ideal temperatures are between 125°F and 135°F. Anything over 140°F and the cheese will just cook. Times will also vary depending on the moisture content. Something like parmesan is already quite dry and can be ready in as little as six hours, but soft cheeses can take up to 12 hours.

You will know the cheese is ready if it's crunchy when you squeeze it. When crunchy, spread the dehydrated cheese on a kitchen towel to remove any excess fat on the surface and then grind it into a powder. The powder can be added to the chili sauce before or after dehydrating.

Chicken and Lentils

Ingredients

- Lentils
- Chicken
- Onion
- Carrots
- Leeks
- Mushrooms
- Garlic
- Bay leaves
- Option 1: Dried mixed herbs (oregano, thyme, parsley) and vegetable stock
- Option 2: Ginger, paprika, chili powder, dried turmeric and coconut milk

Method

As with the other recipes, preparation may depend on what you already have dehydrated. I tend to have everything from the chicken to the garlic already dried. If I am using them dry, I start with stock and herbs (or coconut water and spices for a curry flavor) and lentils and add the dehydrated items. Add the bay leaves, but remove them before serving. Dried lentils take around 35 minutes to cook, which is enough time for the other ingredients to rehydrate and cook.

Alternatively, sauté the onions, carrots, and leeks, adding the mushrooms for the last couple of minutes. Then add the chicken and cook for another 5 minutes, stirring so the chicken is cooked evenly. Again, add the garlic and bay leaves, then either option one or option two, and your lentils.

When the lentils are cooked, there should still be quite a bit of liquid because you don't want to dry them out. Separate the chicken and vegetables from the liquid using a colander. Add the liquid back to the pan and reduce it over low heat. Spread the vegetables and chicken on one rack and the liquid on a tray. Dehydrate at 135°F for 8-10 hours. Check the progress of both during the drying time. If you notice clumps in the lentils, break them up and continue drying. Combine both of the dried ingredients for rehydrating.

FUN FOR THE KIDS

Fruit Powder

Ingredients

You can use a combination of any fruits your little one likes and even sneak in a couple of extras for variety. Here are some ideas that pair well and some herbs and spices for added nutrition:

- Apple, blackberry, plum, cranberry, pear, ginger, nutmeg, cinnamon
- Banana, blueberry, coconut, raspberry, strawberry, cardamom, allspice
- Cherry, fig, orange, plum, black pepper, sage
- Dragon fruit, lemon, lime, mango, pomegranate, mint

- Orange, blueberry, grapefruit, melon, papaya, clove, cumin, anise

Method

The simplest way to make fruit powder is to dry all of the ingredients and add them to a blender to make a powder. This is especially true if you already have a selection of dried fruits. You could also cook different fruits together and make fruit leathers, saving some for a snack and making a powder with the rest.

For adult versions of fruit powders, simmer the fruit in your choice of alcohol. Once the liquid has been reduced, puree and dehydrate to make fruit leathers or grind into a powder.

Powdered fruit can be used in smoothies, on cereal, on ice cream, to flavor milk or yogurt, or as a dip for chocolate, to name a few ideas.

Peanut Butter Balls

Ingredients

- Peanut butter
- Coconut
- Dried apples
- Vanilla
- Tapioca starch or arrowroot powder

Method

Because of the fat content, peanut butter is tricky to dehydrate. Adding a little tapioca starch or arrowroot powder can help bind the fats for better results. Combine all of the ingredients and mix them well. Take a small amount of the mixture and roll it into a small ball.

The peanut butter balls will be crisp and firm on the outside after around 10 hours at 135ºF. For alternative flavors, you can replace the apple with dried banana, raspberries, strawberries, or peaches.

Sweet and Savory Cauliflower Popcorn

Ingredients

- Cauliflower
- Garlic powder
- Onion powder
- Paprika
- Cheese powder
- Olive oil

Method

Cut the cauliflower into bite-sized pieces. Blanching the cauliflower is optional, but if you do blanch it, make sure it's dry before adding other ingredients. Combine all the ingredients in a bowl and add the cauliflower pieces. Mix so that all the pieces are coated in the oil, but only lightly. Place the pieces on a rack and dehydrate for around 10 hours at 115ºF.

Banana and Blueberry Smoothie

Ingredients

- Bananas
- Blueberries
- Chia seeds
- Plain or Greek yogurt
- Milk

Method

Dehydrate the bananas, blueberries, and chia seeds. Don't forget to blanch the blueberries to break the skin. Don't soak the chia seeds before dehydrating them because they will just gel together. Grind the dried bananas and blueberries into a powder. You can leave the chia seeds whole for a different smoothie texture or grind them if you want some extra nutrients that need to be hidden. Mix the powders into the yogurt and then add milk until you get the consistency you like.

Apple Pie Granola

Ingredients

- Apples
- Nuts and seeds of your choice
- Rolled oats
- Raisins
- Cranberries
- Ginger powder
- Nutmeg powder
- Cinnamon powder
- Apple juice

Method

Place the nuts and seeds in a bowl and soak them in water. You may need two bowls if you have a mixture of larger and smaller ingredients or add the smaller ingredients later on. Put the rolled oats in another bowl and soak in a mixture of apple juice and water. The nuts, seeds, and oats will need around 8 hours of soaking but can be left overnight. When these ingredients have finished soaking, add raisins to warm water for around 15 minutes. In the meantime, drain the oats, seeds, and nuts. Patting the nuts and seeds with kitchen paper will help remove extra moisture.

Drain the raisins and blanch the cranberries. Combine all of the prepared ingredients in a bowl and add the spices. Grate the apples, add them to the bowl, and mix well. Spread the granola mixture onto a tray or rack with a cookie sheet and dehydrate at 115°F. If you prefer gooey granola, it will take about 8 hours but if you like crunchy granola, it can take up to 18 hours.

SOMETHING SWEET

Smores

Ingredients

- Buckwheat groats
- Cashews
- Oats
- Cinnamon
- Nutmeg
- Maple syrup
- Prunes/figs/dates

Method

Begin by adding equal amounts of buckwheat, cashews, and oats to a blender and mixing them until they have the consistency of flour. Mix in the cinnamon and nutmeg. Add your prunes, figs, or dates and blend again. The ingredients will start to clump together. Add enough maple syrup to make the ingredients into a dough. Roll the dough out so it's about ¼ inch thick and cut into squares. Place the squares on a tray and dehydrate at 110°F for approximately 3 hours.

It's best to assemble the smores when the cookies are still warm or, if you are feeling adventurous, turn the temperature of your dehydrator down and add the marshmallows and chocolate. Marshmallows will puff up slightly, and the chocolate will melt over the top.

Fruity Muffins

Ingredients

As we are baking, I have included the exact amounts for the muffins.

- 2 cups of whole wheat flour
- 1 cup of milk
- ¾ cup of white sugar
- ¾ cup of butter
- 3 teaspoons of baking powder
- ½ teaspoon of baking powder
- 2 eggs

Method for muffin batter

Cut the butter into cubes and allow to soften. Mix all of the dry ingredients and then add the butter, using a fork to work the butter in until the mixture appears like breadcrumbs. Next, add the wet ingredients and continue mixing until you have a smooth batter.

Ideas for dried fruit

- Apricots
- Banana
- Blueberries
- Cranberries
- Cherries

- Oranges
- Plums
- Prunes
- Raisins
- Raspberries
- Strawberries

Muffins are perfect for adding ingredients that you have already dehydrated and stored. You can choose one fruit or combine several. To add dried fruits to the muffin batter, try to make sure the pieces are all a similar size. Rehydrate the pieces in water, juice, or alcohol and mix them into the batter. Bake the muffins in a preheated oven at 180°F for 20-25 minutes.

Macadamia Balls

Ingredients

- Macadamias
- Shredded coconut
- Milk
- Maple syrup
- Cocoa powder
- Vanilla extract
- Sea salt

Method

With the coconut and milk, we are going to make coconut cream, which can be done in advance. Remove the flesh from the coconut and put it in a blender. Blend on a high speed to shred it. Add milk and blend again so that the two are well combined. Pour the contents into a cheesecloth and squeeze out all the liquid. Don't throw away the pulp because you can dehydrate it at 115°F for 4-5 hours. With the remaining liquid, set it aside for a while until you see the lighter liquid separate from the coconut cream. Remove the liquid and preserve the cream.

We want the macadamias to retain their texture, so don't soak them; instead, freeze them for 15 minutes to prevent them from turning into butter. Next, add the macadamias to a blender and process them until they are ground. Add some of the dehydrated coconut pulp, maple syrup, cocoa powder, vanilla extract, and sea salt. Finally, gradually add some coconut cream and pulse until the ingredients combine into a slightly sticky ball.

Make small balls with the mixture and roll them in the coconut pulp. Place the balls on a tray and dehydrate them at 130°F for 12-18 hours.

Carrot and Cranberry Scones

Ingredients

- Carrots
- Cranberries
- Apples
- Raisins
- Hazelnuts
- Flax seeds
- Ginger
- Maple syrup

Method

Use a juicer to make pulp out of the carrots. If you don't have a juicer, blend the carrots on high speed with water and then use a cheesecloth to squeeze out the moisture. Also, blend the hazelnuts to get flour consistency. Grate the apples, or if you have dehydrated grated apples, rehydrate some. Soak the flax seeds in water. Normally, you don't want to soak flax seeds because they gel, but this will help hold the scones together. You can choose whether or not to rehydrate the raisins and cranberries. Ginger can also be added fresh or dried.

Once all of your ingredients are prepared, mix them together. Take a small handful and shape it into a scone. Place the scones on a tray and dehydrate at 115°F for around 7 hours. Halfway through the drying, turn the scones over.

Berries and Cream Pie

Ingredients

- Dried strawberries
- Dried raspberries
- Dried blueberries
- Alcohol (prosecco, whiskey, or a berry liquor as examples)
- 1 packet of powdered gelatine
- Icing sugar
- Lemon juice
- Cardamon
- Allspice
- Whipped cream

For the pie crust

- 1 ½ cups of flour
- ½ cup of butter
- 1 tablespoon of sugar

- ½ teaspoon of salt
- ½ cup of cold water

Method

Starting with the pie crust, mix the flour, butter, sugar, and salt with your hands. Gradually add the cold water until you have a ball of dough. Cover with cling film and leave it in the fridge for 30 minutes. Roll the dough out and place it in a pie dish. Cover it with aluminum foil and baking beans or rice, if you don't have beans, this will prevent the pie crust from rising. Cook the pie crust at 350°F for 30 minutes. Carefully remove the beans, and if the pie crust isn't completely cooked, put it back in the oven until it's golden brown. Remove from the oven and leave to cool.

Rehydrate the dried berries either by simmering in alcohol or water, if you prefer. Add the gelatine and mix the berries until it dissolves. Add the lemon juice, cardamom, and allspice. Leave the mixture to cool to room temperature before pouring it into the pie crust. Sprinkle a little icing sugar into the whipped cream and whip it until firm. Spoon the cream onto the pie and refrigerate for 1 hour.

I hope these recipes inspire you. My intention wasn't to create a cookbook, which is why there are few specific instructions. The goals of these recipes are to show you how much can be achieved with dehydrated ingredients and to encourage you to experiment with the extensive range of flavors you can achieve. Speaking of flavors, nothing adds a spark to a dish quite like herbs and spices, which is where we will begin in the next step of our DEHYDRATE method.

7

A—ADVANCED DEHYDRATION SKILLS

"Imagine walking out of a grocery store with four grocery bags, dropping one in the parking lot, and just not bothering to pick it up. That's essentially what we are doing."

— DANA GUNDERS

Apart from ensuring you and your family are fully prepared, dehydrating food is an excellent way to reduce food waste. The more skills you have under your belt, the less waste your household can produce, which is good for the pocket and the planet. In this chapter, we will take things to the next level by enhancing flavors and exploring other skills and techniques to improve texture and health benefits. Though we have touched on drying herbs and spices, let's begin here.

MAKING YOUR OWN HERB AND SPICE MIXES

Herbs are great to dry in a dehydrator because the process is fast. If you are harvesting your own herbs, the best time is just before the flowers start to open in the morning, when the dew has dried. This is the ideal moment for both nutritional value and flavor. Rinse the herbs under water and gently shake them to remove moisture. For your hardy herbs, you can lightly pat them, but for tender herbs, you risk bruising the leaves. Remove any damaged leaves and long stems, and spread the herbs on trays. Don't dry herbs at temperatures of more than 100°F because this is when they start to lose their flavor. Depending on the herb type, they will be dry between 1-4 hours.

Spices come from the seeds, bark, and roots, so how you prepare your spices will vary. Seeds like coriander, cardamom, and mustard can be spread on cookie sheets and, again, dehydrated at a temperature of no more than 100°F.

Chilis, though technically fruit, can be made into chili powder once they are dehydrated. You can leave the chilis whole, but they will take longer, so I slice them in half. Wear gloves or, at the very least, wash your hands right after preparing them. Peppers for paprika can be sliced and dehydrated at the same time. Because they are fruits, temperatures will need to be higher, at 145°F, and it can take 6-10 hours to fully dry them.

For root spices, such as ginger and turmeric, cut them into even slices and lay them on a tray. The slices are best dehydrated at 105°F for 2-4 hours, but if you are doing a batch of herbs and spices, keep the temperature below 100°F and expect the slices to take a little longer.

Garlic is the other popular choice for creating your own spice powder, but a word of warning: the smell of garlic as it dries can fill your entire house, so you may want to move your dehydrator outside. Also, this is the only time I ever dehydrate other foods at the same time that I would use when cooking with garlic. For example, dehydrating onions and garlic at the same time can be beneficial, especially because of the strong smell of onions. Typically, garlic is dried at a lower temperature than onions, but I found that 115°F is a good midpoint to dry them both for 8-10 hours. Honestly, homemade ground garlic powder is the best I have ever tasted.

Dried herbs and spices can be kept for 3-5 years in airtight containers (I found glass jars to be the best) with no additional storage techniques needed. Because they are often used in less quantities than other dried foods, they are also likely to last longer. For this, you need to ensure that they are completely dried because any remaining moisture can spoil years' worth of flavors. All herbs and spices should snap when dried. For storage, you can crumble herbs between your fingers. Spices can be kept whole or ground into a powder using a coffee or pepper grinder. For things like garlic and chilis, I keep some whole and make a powder with the rest.

There are so many ways to use your herbs and spices, but here are a few recipes to make your own seasonings combining dried herbs and spices. Again, I'm not going to list the exact amounts, but the order of ingredients goes from higher to lower quantities.

Taco Seasoning

- Chili powder
- Ground cumin
- Onion powder
- Garlic powder

- Sea salt
- Oregano
- Paprika
- Pepper

Curry Powder

- Paprika
- Ground cumin
- Ground turmeric
- Ground coriander
- Ginger powder
- Ground mustard seeds
- Cinnamon powder
- Ground cloves

Italian Seasoning

- Dried basil
- Dried oregano
- Dried marjoram (or sage)
- Dried rosemary
- Dried thyme
- Dried parsley
- Garlic powder (optional)

Cajun Seasoning

- Paprika
- Garlic powder
- Ground cumin
- Salt

- Onion powder
- Chili powder
- Italian seasoning
- Black pepper

Ranch Dressing

- Dried parsley
- Dried chives
- Dried dill
- Garlic powder
- Dried oregano
- Salt
- Chili powder (optional)
- Paprika (optional)

For the dressing, combine mayonnaise, sour cream, and milk to get the desired consistency.

For each of these seasonings, you may need to run the combined ingredients through a coffee grinder or blender so that the consistency of each herb and spice is the same. If not, you may end up with larger pieces of herbs compared with the finer powder of the spices. Don't forget to label your seasonings with the dates you originally dried each ingredient and store your jars in a cool, dark place for better preservation.

MASTERING TEXTURE CONTROL

Marinating meat is optional, but it definitely improves the texture. Because of the amazing range of ingredients you can use, you get to create jerky with incredibly different flavors. For example, you can marinate chicken in lemon, honey, and garlic, or for a complete alternative, leave the chicken in a mixture of peanut butter, ginger, chili powder, and white wine vinegar.

There is no hard and fast rule for marinating meat, but there are influencing factors. Marinating times can be anywhere from 4-6 hours up to 24 hours. Tougher meats like beef need longer, but fish would only need a few hours. The thickness of the meat also influences marinating times. Thicker slices will need longer for the ingredients to absorb fully. Results can also vary based on the direction in which you cut the meat. If you want a tender jerky, cut against the grain, and if you prefer a slightly chewier texture, cut with the grain (Inbound Pursuit 2024).

You might be tempted to leave meat marinating for longer times for more flavor, but there is always a possibility of over-marinating food. This will lead to a mushy, soft texture and maybe even too strong a flavor. The idea of marinating is to enhance flavors but not to lose the natural flavors of the meat you choose.

The base of most marinades is a sauce, such as soy or Worcestershire, and herbs and spices of your choice. Salt and sugar are often used to further improve the flavor, and these two ingredients help with moisture extraction. To tenderize meat and break down proteins, you also need an acidic component, typically vinegar or citric juice.

An alternative to marinades is a dry rub. Dry rubs are a combination of herbs and spices that are rubbed straight onto the meat before cooking. The advantage of a dry rub is that it doesn't add additional moisture to your meat. At the same time, it doesn't tenderize the meat the same way a liquid marinade would. Nevertheless, during my research, I came across an interesting recipe that involved dehydrating a marinade to make a dry rub, with impressive results that were tested by professionals in the catering industry.

The researchers were quite specific about the ingredients, and I followed the recipe as closely as I could, considering they gave the ratio as optimal percentages.

- Fresh ripe papaya puree- 34%
- Raw onion puree- 33%
- Fresh tomato puree- 18%
- Fresh garlic puree- 6%
- Salt- 5%
- Lemon juice- 1.8%
- Chili powder- 1%
- Black pepper powder- 0.5%
- Lemon zest- 0.5%
- Stevia- 0.2%

(Kohli 2018)

Once you have mixed the ingredients, weigh them because you will need to add an equal weight of water and then boil the ingredients for four hours. After boiling, drain the ingredients through a cheesecloth. Spread the solid ingredients on a tray and dehydrate at 120°F for 15 to 20 hours. You will end up with a granular mixture.

What makes this dry rub uniquely effective is the papaya. Papaya contains an enzyme called papain. This enzyme breaks down muscle fiber proteins and connective tissues by adding a water molecule to the proteins, a process called hydrolysis (Kohli 2018). Furthermore, this enzyme is active in hot temperatures, so meat continues to tenderize during the cooking process.

For improved texture with fruits and vegetables, we have discussed techniques such as pretreating and blanching. Marinating fruit and vegetables won't enhance the texture, but you can imagine how much you can alter flavors with your herbs and spices. For example, with kale and cucumber chips, you can try adding garlic, cilantro, dill, or oregano.

Another way to play around with textures is by partial rehydration. If you feel like your fruit slices are too crispy, you can soak them for less than the recommended time. Even just a few minutes can turn a crispy apple slice into a chewy one. For vegetables, pay close attention to the amount of time you blanch them and the impact on the texture. It doesn't sound like a lot, but one minute can make a big difference. The same can be said about rehydration times before cooking your vegetables. Before following strict timings, follow your taste buds and try food throughout the rehydration process.

If you are looking to make your jerky a little softer, you can place it in a microwavable container with the lid over the top but not sealed. Add a glass of water and microwave for one minute at a time until you get the desired texture. This is best if you are planning to eat the jerky fairly soon because once it cools, it will go hard again. Marinades, sauces, and stocks can be used to partially rehydrate jerky, but you don't want to leave it for too long or let it soak in any liquid as it can turn mushy. Instead, use a brush to add a little moisture and leave it for up to 24 hours.

It might feel like mastering texture control is a little overwhelming, but you will get the hang of it sooner than you think. Don't forget to take notes on the effects of marinating, not just on texture but also on the flavors you achieve. These notes with the details will help you constantly improve.

WHY COMBINE FERMENTATION WITH DEHYDRATION

Fermentation has long been used as a method of food preservation. In fact, the Aztecs would soak seeds in brine (salt water) before sun-drying them (Pope n.d.). It's a process where bacteria, yeast, or fungi convert sugars and starch into acids or alcohol. The acids and alcohol not only preserve food but also enhance flavors. There are additional health benefits to adding fermented food to your diet.

The first benefit is that fermented food is essential for healthy bacteria, with both probiotics and prebiotics. Probiotics help restore balance in the gut, whereas prebiotics are a source of food for healthy bacteria. Previously, we saw how antinutrients such as phytic acid prevent the absorption of some vitamins and minerals. Fermentation removes these antinutrients, so the body is better able to absorb all the health benefits in food.

Processed foods have been linked to depression, but on the other hand, a healthy gut microbe has a significant connection to improved mental health. The human stomach is often referred to as the second brain, thanks to the connection between the brain and the gut through the vagus nerve. The two-way communication is what causes butterflies in your stomach when you are nervous. Most of us may assume that the hormones that cause our emotions are created in the brain. While this is true to an extent, remember that 95 percent of the body's serotonin (the hormone associated with happiness and calmness) is produced in the gut (Appleton 2018). What you feed your gut can have a significant impact on mood, anxiety, and depression.

Plenty of different foods can be fermented, but at this point, we will stick to those that are related to our dehydration techniques. Before delving into specifics, it's good to know a little about which method to choose. We will look at two simple methods that can be done at home: wet brine and dry brine. Both require salt, but wet brine also requires water. Lactic fermentation requires salt because the salt kills the bad bacteria and encourages Lactobacillus bacteria, which converts sugars and fruits into lactic acid.

While you can choose either wet or dry brine, generally speaking, we want to keep the moisture content low, so I only use wet brine for food with low moisture content. Let's use sauerkraut as our first example. All you need to make sauerkraut is a jar with a lid, cabbage, and salt. Begin by weighing your cabbage, as you need 2 percent of the cabbage's weight in salt (Newman & Morimoto 2024). Chop the cabbage into thin strips and place them in a bowl. Take the salt and massage the cabbage strips with the salt. You will start to notice moisture being released from the cabbage. Pour all the contents of the bowl into a jar and use a knife to push all the cabbage below the brine. For lactic fermentation to work, there can't be any oxygen. Seal the jar and keep an eye on it over the following days. When you start to see bubbles forming, you need to open the jar to release the buildup of gas. Typically, fermentation will take around two weeks, but this could be less in warmer conditions. As you approach the two weeks, taste the sauerkraut and leave it for longer, depending on your tastes.

For wet brining, the amount of salt varies depending on the food. Firm food (for example: broccoli, cauliflower, carrots, and garlic) may need between 15-30 grams of salt per liter, whereas softer food (think: cucumbers, peppers, and zucchini) needs closer to 50 grams per liter of water (Le Cordon Bleu n.d.). Again, this will depend on your preferences. The process is very much the same. You can cut larger fruits and vegetables or leave them whole. Mix the salt and water, and add the ingredients so that they are fully submerged in the brine. Don't forget to open the jar to release the gas.

Fermenting meat is possible, but it requires additional ingredients because, as we saw with dehydration, meat has no sugars. Begin by using fresh, high-quality meat and cut off any fat. You can cut the meat into smaller pieces, but don't spend too long on this. You want the meat to stay as cold as possible so that bacteria don't have the chance to grow. You can add herbs and spices to the meat to experiment with flavor. Along with your salt brine, add sugar and some form of acidic liquid such as vinegar or lemon juice. I strongly recommend you follow the exact fermenting recipes to ensure your meat is safe, especially when it comes to temperature.

Once you have fermented your food, try to remove as much moisture as possible before dehydrating. Also, bear in mind that, especially after using a wet brine, dehydration times may be longer. Keep a closer eye on the process when you get to the end of the drying times.

WHEN FREEZE DRYING MAKES SENSE

Freeze drying is a three-part process that is ideal for raw fruits, vegetables, and meats because of the high water content. Water can be either free or bound. Free water will freeze, but bound water won't, which is why there are multiple stages. It's a technique that turns moisture into ice and then vapor without going through the liquid state. In the first stage, food is frozen under atmospheric pressure. During the primary drying stage, the frozen water is removed. The final secondary drying stage removes the bound water that wasn't frozen.

One of the main reasons to freeze-dry food is for the additional health benefits. Studies have shown that freeze-drying retains more antioxidants than other dehydrating methods (Lang 2024). The increased shelf life and preserved color and flavor are also benefits achieved by freeze-drying. The other good news is that the same range of foods that you would dehydrate in an oven, air fryer, or dehydrator can be freeze-dried.

You might be wondering why we didn't begin with freeze-drying if it's considered one of the best preservation methods. The main reason for this is the cost. To freeze dry food, you need highly specific equipment, including a vacuum pump. An oil pump can cost around $200, but you will also need oil filters and regular maintenance. An oil-less vacuum pump might set you back around $1,700, and you will still need other equipment like a vacuum sealer or oxygen absorber. However, a freeze-dryer machine can be anywhere from $2,000 upwards (USU Extension n.d.).

Please be careful of sites that tell you that you can freeze dry food with your freezer. Yes, you can slice food and lay it on cookie sheets to freeze, and then put the frozen slices in a vacuum-sealing bag to seal it. A vacuum sealer will remove air from the bag and, therefore, moisture in the bag, but not from the food itself. Also, because the moisture isn't removed from the food, it doesn't make it safe to eat. Food will still need cooking, unlike your delicious fruit and vegetable chips and jerky. Nevertheless, this is still an advanced dehydration method you might want to consider using in the future.

In summary, these techniques are ideal building blocks to take dehydrated food to the next level. From my own experience, in terms of food preparation, health benefits, and environmentally friendly practices, I try to grow as much of my own food as possible. I'm certainly not suggesting you start growing all of your food because, like dehydration, it's something best started slowly and added to. I recommend starting with herbs because they are some of the easiest things to grow. Peppers and chilis are also perfect for beginners, and you can get an impressive yield for preservation.

When it comes to adding flavor, whether that's with marinating or during fermentation, sometimes less is more. With marinating, it's easy to get carried away and add a bit of this and an extra dash of that, but the goal is not to mask the natural flavors that come with dehydrating your food. Fermentation can create an entirely different set of flavors, from sour to tangy, and again, the flavors you add should be subtle. Think of it the same way you would when cooking. A dish that lacks flavor can be added to, but as soon as you go over the top, it's a challenge to correct overpowerful flavors. You risk wasting the food, which goes against our main purpose. The worst that can happen if you don't add enough flavor is that you can add more during the rehydration and cooking processes, or you learn for the next time.

Nobody becomes an expert overnight, especially when there are so many variables. In the penultimate step of the DEHYDRATE method, we will cover what to do when things don't go as planned.

8

T—TROUBLESHOOTING TIPS

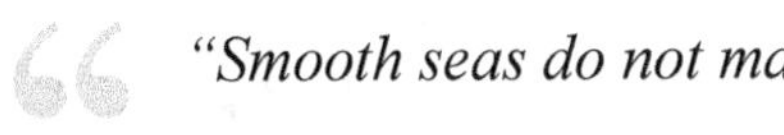 *"Smooth seas do not make skillful sailors."*

— AFRICAN PROVERB

It's the perfect proverb that highlights the need for plenty of practice in order to master any skill. Without challenges along the way, you won't be able to improve your techniques. Some of the troubleshooting tips in this chapter have already been mentioned, but since we have covered a lot of ground, I wanted this chapter to be more of a quick reference guide to easily overcome any obstacles you face.

COMMON DEHYDRATION TROUBLESHOOTING

Please always remember food safety first. In some cases, you will still be able to eat the food although the flavor might not tickle your tastebuds. In other cases, it's best to discard the food.

Food doesn't dehydrate

Pieces might be too large or overlapping in the dehydrator. You may also have a problem with a lack of air circulation. Trays that aren't in use should always be removed for better airflow. Unless your dehydrator specifies otherwise, your food may benefit from rotating the trays.

Food darkens or has dark spots

If food darkens or you see brown spots, it's because of the Maillard reaction. This is where amino acids and some simple sugars are rearranged during cooking (Modernist Cuisine 2013). It's what gives certain foods their distinct flavor and aroma when roasting, frying, or baking. You might already guess why your dehydrated food has brown spots. The temperatures are too high, and the food is being cooked rather than dehydrated. Reduce the temperature and pay closer attention towards the end of the drying time.

Food takes too long

High moisture content is the obvious reason for longer drying times, and this can be helped by increasing the drying temperature but not above the recommended maximum temperature. Double-check that your slices are even, and consider how you are preparing your food. You might want to try steam balancing or slightly reducing the time you water blanch. With regards to the dehydrator, as much as you want to maximize your space, try not to overload the trays because this can negatively impact air circulation. Dehydrators with a top or bottom-mounted fan tend to take longer to dry food, so it makes sense to rotate your trays if your fan isn't back-mounted.

Potatoes go brown

Brown potatoes are caused by oxidation, so a good rule of thumb is to make sure they are always in water to prevent oxygen from interacting with the slices. Have a bowl of cold water ready for peeled and sliced potatoes, and another cold bowl of water ready for after balancing or partially cooking them. For faster draining, I use two colanders for larger amounts of potato slices. Skipping the blanching stage is another reason for potatoes to go brown.

Mushrooms go black

Black mushrooms, unfortunately, can't be saved, but you can prevent this from happening with the correct preparation. If a mushroom has been frozen prior to dehydrating, it will more likely spoil. This goes for mushrooms that may have been frozen before picking, too. Unlike other fruits and vegetables that are better dehydrated when ripe, mushrooms are best when they are fresh. To test this, when you break the stem, you should hear a tiny snap. Any signs of damage, such as spots, slimy texture, or if a mushroom bends instead of breaks, means it's not suitable for dehydration.

Meat and fish don't dry

The most likely cause of meat or fish not drying is the thickness of the slices, which is why I highly recommend a meat slicer or mandolin with a meat slicer attachment for uniform slices. Be careful not to over-marinate fish or meat, as this will lead to mushy results that don't dehydrate well. Dry rubs can be highly effective for texture and flavor.

Jerky is chewy

To an extent, jerky should turn out chewy if that's the desired texture you are going for. When the chewiness ruins the experience, and it's impossible to eat, there is an issue. This unpleasant chewiness is likely due to fat on the meat before dehydration. Even if you choose the leanest parts of meat, be sure to cut any excess fat you can see. Choose cuts of meat with more marbling or intramuscular fat. This fat runs between the muscle fibers and can help improve texture. For more tender jerky, you can massage the meat to help relax the muscle fibers and vacuum seal the meat when it's marinating. Vacuum sealing meat separates fibers and increases the amount of contact the marinade has with the meat.

Food tastes off

There are two possibilities for food not tasting right. The first is that you have dehydrated foods together that transfer flavors. For example, if you dehydrate a curry along with a tomato sauce, you may notice hints of curry in the tomato sauce. Sometimes, this isn't a problem. For example, I quite like a hint of curry with my lentils but not with a spaghetti Bolognese. A good rule of thumb is to dehydrate foods from the same family together and be sure to dehydrate things like onions, garlic, and chilies separately. Another reason that food might taste off is that some food residue might be left on the inside of your dehydrator, which we will cover in the section on dehydrator maintenance.

Food is sticking

It's only normal that there are going to be some sticky residues when you consider the sugars, especially in fruit. Pretreating food can help reduce the stickiness. Otherwise, cleaning up is easier when you use non-stick trays, cookie sheets, or a very light spray of cooking oil. Food that has stuck might not be pretty, but it will still be edible.

Food is crispy on the outside but moist inside

Case hardening is when food is dehydrated at temperatures that are too high. The outer surface develops a hard coating that prevents moisture from the inside from escaping. This is common with things like berries, peas, and corn when the skin isn't broken, and moisture can't escape. You need to either blanch these foods or slice them a few times. Temperatures play an important role in preventing case hardening. You may want to set the dehydrator at a temperature of 5°F to 10°F higher for the first hour to remove surface moisture and then lower the temperature for the remaining drying time. This is where a dehydrator with dual temperature settings can come in handy. Case hardening isn't the same as dehydrated food that still has moisture in it. For the latter, you need more drying time whereas with case hardening, more time won't make a difference. While you can still eat food that has suffered hard casing, you won't get that crispy texture you might have been expecting.

Moisture in the jars or container

Food with case hardening can't be stored in jars because the moisture in the food will end up trapped in the jar. You may also notice moisture in the jar if you have left food to cool for too long before storing it. When food is left at room temperature, it can absorb moisture from the air. It's necessary to store dehydrated food as soon as it has cooled. Check your containers within the first week of storage. If you see any moisture, the food will need to be dehydrated again.

Mold on food

This is a nightmare for any dehydrator because there is no saving food once it has gone moldy. Mold is caused by moisture in the jar or container either because it hasn't been dehydrated properly, case hardening, not storing it quickly enough, or your container isn't airtight. Test various pieces on a tray to ensure all the food is properly dehydrated, and test from different shelves, too. Even after checking the container for moisture in the first week, make sure all containers are stored in a cool area of your home, ideally below 70°F (Pick Your Own n.d.).

As you can see, the majority of the issues that come about when dehydrating food are because of incorrect temperatures or insufficient drying times, which are easy fixes. When these two problems are under control, you significantly reduce the risk of other challenges that may arise with storage and preservation.

HOW DOES ALTITUDE IMPACT DEHYDRATION?

If you are using a dehydrator, air fryer, or oven, altitude won't impact the dehydration of food, but it is something to be aware of if you are sun-drying or air-drying. High altitudes mean the air is thinner, there is less oxygen, and moisture evaporates more quickly, so you can expect drying times to be less the higher above sea level you are.

The altitude is going to have a bigger impact on your rehydration and cooking of your dehydrated food. One of the biggest considerations is that water boils at 208°F at altitudes of more than 2,000 feet above sea level compared with 212°F at lower altitudes (Food Safety and Inspection Service 2024). You then have to factor in faster evaporation rates. You can see how rehydration and cooking can become a new challenge. Whether you live at a high altitude or are a fan of hiking in the great outdoors, there are some helpful calculations to create delicious, rehydrated (and safe) meals.

Let's tackle the problem of rehydrating and water quantities first because it's the easiest. On the one hand, you can use a sealed container, as the water won't evaporate. This makes it relatively simple to check the rehydration process. Alternatively, you may just need to keep a closer eye on the amount of water that evaporates and adjust accordingly.

Next, we can look at the additional hot soak time dehydrated food will need considering drops in boiling temperature at different altitudes. For this purpose, we will work on the theory that at sea level water boils at 212°F and won't need more than the recommended hot water soaking time. Here is a rough guide on what to expect.

Seal Level in Feet	Boiling Temperature	Additional Soak Time
5,000	203°F	1 minute
7,500	198°F	2 minutes
10,000	194°F	5 minutes
20,000	178°F	15 minutes

(Outdoor Herbivore Blog 2019)

Altitudes of more than 20,000 are uncommon, but please also bear in mind that cooking at these heights requires specialist equipment like a portable pressure cooker. Nevertheless, if you don't make adjustments, you will start to notice more of a difference once you pass 5,000 feet above sea level.

Moving on to cooking with your dehydrated food; you will also need a couple of extra calculations. First, you will have to deal with water evaporation during the cooking process. This is easily resolved if you are cooking with a lid. If not, you may need to gradually add more water. For every cup of water you added at the beginning of the cooking stage, you will need to add an additional 2 tablespoons of water for every 5,000 feet gain in altitude. It doesn't sound like much, but it could be enough to stop your noodles and pasta from being too crunchy.

Along with adjusting for water evaporation, your cooking times may need to be slightly tweaked as soon as you are above 2,000 feet. Another handy rule of thumb is to increase the cooking time by 5 percent for each 1,000 feet of elevation. So, at 3,000 feet, you would increase the cooking time by 5 percent (or multiply it by 1.05); at 4,000 feet, it's a 10 percent increase (or multiply it by 1.10); at 5,000 feet, you would need 15 percent (or multiply it by 1.15); and so on (Healthy Instant Pot n.d.).

You might think this is off-topic for a book on dehydrating food, but in terms of being prepared for any situation, it's important to take the environmental conditions into consideration. It's not always about hiking or camping; sometimes, on a sunny day it's fun and healthier to cook outdoors in your garden. With the rise of natural disasters, you may have noticed an increase in power outages, and conventional cooking methods won't be available. So, these small adjustments are necessary for completing the dehydration experience as well as for self-sufficiency.

FOOD DEHYDRATOR MAINTENANCE

A food dehydrator is a decent investment, and by now, you will probably appreciate how much you will be using it. Cleaning and maintenance are necessary to prevent the transfer of flavors and prolong the longevity of your machine. There are things you can do to make cleaning up easier, such as placing a fresh sheet of cookie paper, but that's only going to catch drips. Even so, it's worth folding the sheet and tucking it under the back screen or finding any way to keep it in place. Once, my cookie sheet flew up toward the fan without me knowing, which was a fun mess to clean.

You should clean the trays after every use. It's often enough to soak them in warm soapy water, but if that's not enough, you can use a non-abrasive sponge. This might sound a little excessive, but it might be worth getting a large bucket for the trays. This is especially true if your trays don't fit in the kitchen sink. It doesn't have to be a long job, but it soon will be if you need to spin each tray to make sure it's clean. A larger bucket allows trays to soak out of the way, for longer if need be. Make sure the trays are fully dried before replacing them in the dehydrator.

I know many dehydrators have trays that are dishwasher safe, but the drying cycle can produce high temperatures that lead to warping of the trays. While this doesn't affect the safety of the food, it can be frustrating. If possible, remove them from the dishwasher before the drying cycle begins or stick to hand washing and leave them to dry naturally.

Cleaning the inside of the dehydrator will depend on how much you use it and the types of food you dry. A good tip is to keep food away from the outer rim of trays, as this will help keep the sides of the dehydrator clean. At the very least, wipe down the sides of the dehydrator once the trays have been removed. It's best to do this when the machine starts to cool but isn't completely cold, and food debris has solidified. Finally, wipe down the outer sides and control panel to remove any dust, debris, and sticky fingerprints.

Apart from the basic cleaning after every use, there should also be some deep cleaning. If you have a vacuum with a fine nozzle, this is an excellent tool to remove crumbs in hard-to-reach places like behind the screen that protects the fan. Alternatively, you can use a steam cleaner that will blast away these crumbs, but you will still need to wipe them away. Q-tips and toothbrushes are great scrubbing tools for smaller gaps, such as the ridges where shelves sit. Try to avoid harsh chemicals inside the dehydrator; soapy water and a little elbow grease should suffice. If that's not enough, you can try making a paste from vinegar and baking soda.

If you are using an oven to dehydrate food, the cleaning process will be the same. It's best to remove the turntable in a microwave, and wipe the inside with warm, soapy water. For air fryers, you can add some warm, soapy water to the basket, and set the timer for three or four minutes. Leave doors open until they are completely dry, and this will help any lingering smells disappear.

You can also use the maintenance checklist to ensure your dehydrator runs at optimal levels for years to come.

- Check for any worn parts and replace them as soon as possible.
- Check the air vents for anything that might block airflow and clean them.
- Check the air filters and replace them according to the manual.
- Check the screws and bolts, and tighten any that are loose.
- Lubricate moving parts such as door hinges.
- Store your dehydrator in a clean and dry environment away from direct sunlight.

Cleaning and maintenance might not be the most glamorous part of food dehydration, but they can greatly reduce potential issues. However, there is something quite therapeutic about watching your vast array of dehydrated foods cool down as you systematically work through the cleaning list, knowing your machine will be ready for your next session.

We have just one chapter left and there we are going to see exactly how to take advantage of your dehydrator year round, and not just for food. It's time to get even more creative!

9

E—EXPERIMENT AND ENJOY

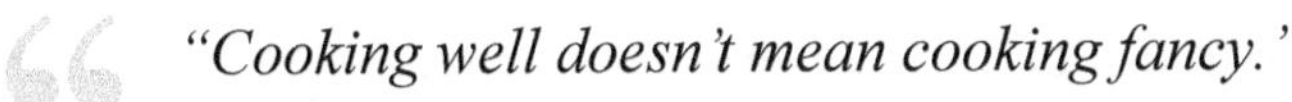

"Cooking well doesn't mean cooking fancy."

— JULIA CHILD

I am a huge fan of herbs and spices, but sometimes, it's worth remembering the wonderfully hearty meals our grandparents and maybe even great-grandparents used to make. They didn't have any fancy cooking techniques or access to exotic flavors. What made their food so nutritious and still delicious was the fact they used fresh ingredients that were in season, something that perhaps we don't always respect today when everything is available year-round.

SEASONAL FOOD GUIDE

Because we are used to seeing most fruits and vegetables on grocery store shelves all year, it's easy to forget which are actually in season and which aren't. You can make fresh orange juice from oranges in summer, and it might be refreshing, but it won't come close to the flavor of orange juice made from oranges in winter months when they are actually in season. The same can be said for all of the fruit and vegetables you dehydrate. The best garlic powder will come from garlic that has been harvested from September to November.

Fresh food is higher in nutritional value. During transportation, foods often must be chilled and then heated in order to force them to finish ripening, causing levels of antioxidants to decrease as well as impacting flavor and texture. Let's not forget the impact the long transportation of food has on the environment. Seasonal food has had the time to complete its natural lifecycle in ideal conditions.

Something else that is often overlooked is that seasonal foods contain specific things our bodies need for that time of the year. For example, summer fruits have high water content to help replenish what we lose in the heat, and they have more vitamin A that can help protect the skin from damage from the sun's rays. On the other hand, winter foods are often higher in vitamin C and D, which can help compensate for the lack of sun (Baranda n.d.).

With reduced transportation and intervention to keep food fresh, seasonal food is often cheaper. You may find that local farmers have good prices. Buying local products cuts out the middleman, and you know more about where your food has come from. Buying locally encourages sustainability and supports the local community without an obsessive amount of plastic wrapping.

Without a few shocking statistics, the need for local and organic shopping may not be fully appreciated. It's estimated that the long-distance transportation of food from farm to plate can be thousands of miles. For greens, it's "only" 889 miles, tomatoes 1,369 miles, and the apple that you bite into may have traveled 1,555 miles (Foodwise n.d.).

The Environmental Working Group publishes an annual report with an analysis of fruits and vegetables that contain the most pesticides. More than 90 percent of strawberries, apples, cherries, spinach, nectarines, and grapes that were tested contained residues of two or more pesticides (Environmental Working Group 2024).

It's not just fruits and vegetables that have their ideal seasons. A wild animal that hibernates during the winter months isn't going to have the same muscle as when they are eating, exercising, and breeding. Even farm-breed animals are subjected to different factors that make meat seasonal, such as the grass quality, heat and rain that can cause stress, and breeding cycles.

Of course, the moment you combine seasonal shopping with dehydration, you get to reap numerous benefits. Life would be a little boring if you could only eat tasty mushrooms or melons for a few months a year. Whether it's the supermarket, local suppliers, or farmers' markets, fresh and in-season food can be bought, prepared, and dehydrated so that you have access to the nutrients and flavors regardless of the month. It's the perfect and cost-effective way to add variety to your diet and ensure your body gets all the vitamins and minerals it needs.

If you are wondering which foods are in season throughout the year, the following guide can help.

Common Vegetables

Vegetable	Months In Season
Asparagus	March-May
Beans	June-November
Broccoli	March-May and September-November
Cabbage	September-May
Carrots	Year-round
Cauliflower	September-November
Corn	June-August
Kale	September-February
Lettuce	March-May and September-November
Onions	September-May
Parsnips	September-February
Potatoes	September-February
Spinach	March-May and September-November
Summer squash	June-August
Winter squash	September-February

Common Fruits

Fruit	Months In Season
Apples	Year-round but ideally August-October
Apricots	March-August
Bananas	Year-round
Berries	June-August
Cherries	June-August
Coconuts	Year-round
Pineapple	September-May
Grapes	September-November
Lemon	Year-round in good weather
Melons	June-August
Oranges	December-February
Papayas	May-June
Peaches	June-August
Pears	September-February
Peppers	March-September
Plums	June-August
Raspberries	June-August
Strawberries	March-August
Tomatoes	June-August

Meat and Fish

Meat/Fish	Months In Season
Beef	Year-round but ideally December-February
Chicken	Year-round
Cod	May-January
Crab	Year-round but ideally September-November
Goat	December-April
Haddock	June-February
Lamb	August-January
Prawns	September-January
Pork	Year-round but ideally October-December
Rabbit	August-October
Salmon	February-August
Tuna	July-October*
Turkey	April-October
Venison	Year-round**

(Inverclyde Council 2020)

*Bluefin tuna can be caught year-round.

**It will depend on the type of venison (buck, stage, or doe) but it can be found fresh year-round.

Herbs and Spices

Herb/Spice	Months in Season
Most herbs	Year-round*
Basil	June-November
Chives	March-September
Garlic	September-November
Ginger	September-November
Turmeric	September-November

(US. Foods n.d.)

*Most herbs can be harvested year-round but for a larger harvest (up to ⅓ of the plant, it's best to wait until the fall.

There are a few considerations with seasonal food, and similar to preparation and dehydration, nothing is cut and dry. Naturally, the first thing to consider is which hemisphere you are in. These seasonal guides are based on the Northern Hemisphere; for those in the Southern Hemisphere, you would have to work on the contrary.

There is also climate change to consider. On the one hand, climate change can mean longer growing seasons because of the warmer temperatures. Warmer temperatures can also affect pollinating insects and the health of animals that are raised for meat. On the other hand, climate change can also increase air pollution, which affects photosynthesis. When plants don't have the same abilities to produce their own food, growth might be stunted, and they are more susceptible to pests and diseases. Surprisingly, 90 percent of global warming actually occurs in the ocean, so seasons for fish and seafood may very well vary or change with time (NASA n.d.).

That being said, the above charts are still a good guide to narrowing down the best times to buy certain food, taking advantage of the price and enhanced quality. Finally, don't forget that this is a long-term plan. If you are a fan of a particular food, but it's not coming into season for a few months, you don't need to starve yourself of it. It's just about a little organization, so you can combine bulk buying of your favorite food with time to dehydrate it. You can use the chart below to create a 12-month plan for what you hope to achieve. Try to be as specific as possible in the final column. For example, if you plan on dehydrating chiles, include whether you want to keep them whole or make chili powder. Or, if you are drying beef, is it for meals or jerky?

Month	Food Wish List	Dehydration Plans
January		
February		
March		
April		
May		
June		
July		
August		
September		
October		
November		
December		

Remember there is no need to overwhelm yourself and replace every food item you have with things that are in season. The simplest and easiest way to prepare for the future is by doing things gradually, even if it's just a couple of different foods each month.

DEHYDRATION BEYOND FOOD

Whether you have invested money into buying a dehydrator or time into making your own, you want to make sure you get more than the most out of it. Your machine will be working hard to provide for the family, but let's not forget our four-legged family friends. Pet food has seen a ridiculous increase in prices, with dog food alone rising by 45.5 percent since 2020 (TotalVet 2024). Jerky that didn't quite turn out right for you will be the perfect treat for pets. Though, personally, I am not keen on eating other parts of animals, I do appreciate that once an animal has been killed for consumption, nothing should go to waste.

Offal refers to edible animal organs. If you aren't eager to try them yourself, it's highly probable that your pets will. Tripe is a good place to start. The lining of the intestines and the stomach of different animals is cheap to buy and packed with nutrients for your pets. Tripe can be washed, sliced, and dehydrated for around 14 hours at a temperature of 160°F; just watch out for green tripe as this will create a strong smell in your house. The liver, on the other hand, doesn't smell at all and can be dried at the same temperature as the tripe but for 10-12 hours.

The heart is another good option because it is pure muscle with perhaps a little fat on the outside that can be trimmed away. Kidneys may have a little fat on the inside, so it's worth slicing them in half and removing the fat before making thinner slices. Both can be dehydrated at 160°F for around 12 hours.

Pigs' ears, skin, and snout will take longer, but it's still not worth attempting to increase the temperature. Stick to 160°F and allow them approximately 24 hours of drying time. Dogs go crazy for these types of treats, and they keep them entertained for a while. Whether or not you pre-cook meat for dogs is up to you, but I would always play it safe and pre-cook it.

If you want to make your own kibble, you can combine staples like rice and lentils with dog-friendly vegetables such as carrots, pumpkin, squash, sweet potato, and zucchini. Prepare and dehydrate them the same way you would for yourself and break them up into smaller pieces before serving.

If you are looking for ways to improve the atmosphere in your home, your dehydrator can serve two purposes. If you or any family member suffers when the air becomes dry, your dehydrator can double up as a humidifier by putting a large bowl of water inside. Just as the machine would remove moisture from food and disperse it, the dehydrator takes the moisture from the bowl and disperses it into your indoor air.

Potpourri can be made from a number of dried ingredients, including orange and lemon peels or apple skins. Flowers like rose, lavender, and jasmine add scent and color, even when dried. Herbs and spices such as mint, cloves, and cinnamon are all good companions to the jar. Once all the ingredients are dry, add them to a jar with some of your favorite essential oils. Every once in a while, shake the jar or add a few more drops of essential oils to refresh the ingredients. Speaking of peels, to add to your self-sufficiency, you can use dried citrus peels as fire starters, too.

If you can't stand damp clothes around your home, don't dismiss the dehydrator for effective drying. You may find it's cheaper to run your dehydrator to finish smaller items of clothing than it is to run your traditional dryer.

Finally, if you are into crafts and clay work, a dehydrator can lead to better results than leaving your clay to air dry. Leaving clay to air dry can cause cracks or items to split. A dehydrator won't create equal results as a kiln, but if it's a fun hobby for you, save yourself some money and space by using your dehydrator at 15°F instead. To test the clay for dryness, touch it. If your creations feel cold, they still have moisture in them.

Homemade crafts like potpourri and clay work are wonderful gifts, but to finish the chapter, let's take a look at some other ways to creatively use your dehydrator for others.

PERSONAL GIFTS TO SHOW YOU CARE

Coming home with a newborn baby is a joy, but it's hard work. Having a well-stocked pantry is a blessing for quick meals when so much else is going on. Omelets were a go-to meal for us, and this led to having ready-made dehydrated omelet rations. We had a jar with dried mushrooms and bacon, another one with onions and peppers, and a third with spinach and herbs. All it took was 15 minutes of warm soaking while getting the baby off to bed, then mixing in the eggs, and dinner was ready. This became one of our favorite gifts for friends and family who were in the same situation.

In fact, there were many food gifts that were much appreciated, with fruit powders being a top option, closely followed by seasonal mixes. For birthdays, you can create truly unique dehydrated gifts. I had a friend who was keen on aloe vera as part of his diet. So, I dehydrated slices that could be added to salads and ground some more into a powder that he could add to smoothies. It was something that he would never have expected.

We are used to seeing the usual herbal tea flavors like chamomile, mint, and fruits of the forest, but there is nothing stopping you from creating your own tea blend. If you know someone who is particularly susceptible to colds and the flu in winter, you could try combining echinacea, ginger, and peppermint for a soothing tea. Most of us know someone whose stress levels are through the roof, so a calming blend of holy basil, lemon balm, and stinging nettles could help them relax (don't worry, all stings are removed once you blanch the leaves). Why stop there? For coffee lovers, you can buy different fresh beans, dehydrate them, and make their favorite coffee blend. Potpourri can also be personalized to include things that individuals like. For someone who loves nature, you can dehydrate pine needles and add pinecones. Special flowers can be dehydrated and framed along with photos or other memorabilia. Even birthday cakes can be decorated with dehydrated flowers.

Thanksgiving is the time of year to show some of your gratitude with your homemade turkey season rub. Try combining dried ingredients such as thyme, rosemary, oregano, onion powder, garlic powder, and a little paprika. If you are tired of gifting the traditional Christmas presents of socks, your dehydrator can make wonderful gifts and some special treats for your dinner table. Nuts are especially popular at this time of year, and you might consider dehydrating and mixing things like walnuts, hazelnuts, and almonds, all of which are considered to bring good luck in the festive season.

I used to think my family was a little crazy for leaving oranges in stockings until I learned that it goes back to Saint Nicolas generously giving bags of gold coins to a poor father and his three daughters. Oranges are often left in stockings as a symbol of gold coins

(Seaver 2023). Today, I dehydrate orange slices and dip half of the slices in dark chocolate—and not just for the stockings!

As an adult Christmas gift, one of my favorites is a DIY mulled wine kit. Common spices used in mulled wine are ginger, cloves, cinnamon, and nutmeg; dried orange slices are a must, and then you just need a bottle of red wine and some brown sugar. Anise stars aren't necessary, but they are impressive for decorations and add flavor.

How you present your homemade gifts can make all the difference. When it comes to gifting food, you still need to consider safety. Regardless of how soon you think they will use up their gift, it's still sensible to store your gifts in air-tight containers. Ziplock bags aren't the most attractive, but they can be spruced up with ribbons or placed inside muslin bags. This is a good solution for herbs, spices, and seasonings. Larger bags can be used for sweet treats, trail mixes, and fruit and vegetable chips. Decorated boxes can also be used for multiple bags.

You will probably have an extensive collection of mason jars, and these couldn't be better to use for presentation. If you have colored ingredients, such as dried fruit and vegetables, you can layer the items for extra visual appeal. Clothes or brown paper can be added to the top of the jars wrapped in string or ribbons. Pegs can be personalized with names or messages and attached to the decorated lids.

For the final tip on presenting your homemade dehydrated gifts, you can etch glass jars and to my surprise, this was easier than I thought. You will need some materials including a paintbrush, etching cream, and stencils. Stencils can be anything with an adhesive back so you can choose from pre-made stencils or craft vinyl comes in sheets and rolls. You can use this to make your own stencils.

Begin by making sure the jar is clean and completely dry. Place the stencil on the jar and firmly press it down, making sure there are no air bubbles. With a paintbrush, cover the entire stenciled area in etching cream. If you accidentally get some on the glass, wipe it off with an old damp cloth. The instructions on your etching cream might say to leave it for a few minutes, but the best results are often achieved after 20 minutes (The Craft Patch n.d.). Wipe away the etching cream and then rinse the jar off. Then, you can remove the stencil from the jar.

Never in a million years would I have imagined myself etching a mason jar with my best friend's dogs' names and then filling the jar up with dehydrated pig ears. Nor would I have pictured myself etching champagne glasses, filling them with Muslin bags of dehydrated strawberries, and giving them to my parents along with a nice bottle of bubbly for their anniversary.

As much as I have come to rely on my dehydrator for food and preparing for the future, I have also stepped out of my comfort zone and used it in less than traditional ways that have made life more creative and fun while at the same time, introducing others to the endless possibilities that are now at your fingertips.

DON'T DITCH IT—DEHYDRATE IT!

Take a minute to think about how much food you used to throw out and how much money you are now saving. Planning for the future isn't just about making sure you have food for a crisis—it's about making sure you are financially prepared, and everyone could benefit from topping up their savings. Your words could help the next family improve their diet and relieve their financial stress. And all it takes is an honest review!

You might not think that your opinions can make that much of a difference but it's the small acts that we all make that can make the world a better place; one dehydrated meal at a time. Thank you in advance and happy experimenting.

Scan the QR code below*:*

CONCLUSION

There is no doubt that drastic changes must be made to both the American diet and the Western diet. We can't go on accepting 900 daily deaths in the US alone because our diets lack balance and nutritional value. It's scary to consider how many people are walking around with chronic physical and/or mental health conditions because of what they eat. And it's sad to think that anyone isn't living their best lives because they aren't getting sufficient vitamins and minerals.

There are several problems with the concept of "going on a diet." First, there is the risk of trying fad diets that may have some positive results but often don't encompass a truly balanced diet. If you have ever tried going on a diet, you will know that the restrictiveness can be rather boring. So, this can often lead to starting a diet and ending it before the benefits are experienced.

There was never just one intention behind this book. I wanted you to be able to see that dehydrating your own food wasn't about going on a diet, but about making small, healthy changes for the long term. I didn't want you to feel like you were purchasing a dehydrating food recipe book, but I knew that some recipes would be inspiring. Above all, I wanted to make sure that your investment, whether financial or time, would be put to the best and most advantageous of uses. It was these hopes and intentions that led to the creation of the DEHYDRATE method.

We began this epic adventure by getting to know the **D**rying basics. I hope by looking into the science of free radicals and antioxidants, you can see exactly how dried fruit and vegetables can support a balanced diet and reduce the risk of potential health problems. Beyond this, dehydrating food enables you to save money and cut back on food wastage, prepare for a rather uncertain future in today's world, and have a positive impact on the environment. This chapter also allowed us to clear up any misconceptions regarding the safety of dehydrated food. While most foods are perfectly safe to dehydrate, it's those with a high-fat content that should be avoided.

Another common misconception we cleared up in the chapter on **E**quipment and methods was that you need a dehydrating machine to dry food. For centuries, various cultures have been drying food using just air and the sun. Your oven might not be the most cost-effective equipment for drying food, but between that and the microwave, you can get started with dehydrating and more specific temperatures. If you have an air fryer, I loved testing it with smaller food items thanks to the lower temperature ranges. The examples of dehydrators on the market today weren't to encourage you to choose one of them but rather to help you see the range of shapes, materials, and features that are available. My only advice is to make sure the dehydrator you choose is one that suits your needs and complies with food safety regulations (such as BPA-free plastic).

How to Make Your Own Dehydrator was a creative chapter on how you can upcycle common items to build an effective drying machine. All of the techniques were relatively basic, and you don't have to be a DIY master to build one. The beauty of making your own dehydrator is in the customization. You can make one at any size that suits the needs of your family. Upcycling materials is another step toward self-sufficiency and helping the planet.

It might have felt like it took a while to get there, but following a logical process meant that the Y in the DEHYDRATE method saw us getting down to the techniques and tips to get **Y**ield optimization. Pretreating fruit, blanching vegetables, and soaking nuts and seeds help to achieve excellent results consistently. Pre-cooking meat is crucial to make sure you are dehydrating meat safely. Finally, we covered some tips for improved results, and of all of them, the most effective is having uniform slices so that food dries consistently. After a dehydrator, a mandolin may just be your new best friend in the kitchen.

Since one of the intentions of this book was to prepare for the future, it made sense to have a chapter on **D**rying for the long term. Here, we understood the advantages of combining dehydrated food with vacuum sealing for improved shelf life. I can't stress enough the importance of labeling everything that you dehydrate. It might not seem like it at first, but it won't be long before your shelves and freezer are brimming with food, and storing this food correctly can help with organization, especially when you use the first in, first out system. With all of these dehydration and preservation strategies, it was time for **R**ecipes and methods that showed you how to put all those marvelous, dried ingredients to good use, and for more than just jerky.

A personal favorite step of this simple and easy method is the Advanced dehydration skills, which allows you to really start to enhance flavors and texture. You can experiment with dried herbs and spices to create your own seasonings and dry rubs, or you can add these ingredients to marinades. Don't forget the secret ingredient of any meat marinade—papaya! To take your dehydrated food to the next level, you can combine it with fermentation, adding more balance to your diet through probiotics and prebiotics. Maintaining a healthy gut microbiome isn't just good for your digestive system. Your gut plays a significant role in mental health because of the gut-brain axis.

Following the method highlighted in these chapters should reduce the risk of potential problems, but I also felt it would be beneficial to have one chapter dedicated to Troubleshooting tips as a quick reference. The final chapter was a fun chapter that encouraged you to Experiment and enjoy your dehydrator for all that it's capable of, from pet treats to unique and personalized gifts for different occasions.

Throughout the pages and our learning, I have tried to include my own experiences and not just the successes. I have loved the results of all my dried herbs and spices, and I am constantly surprised by the results when I combine them with my own herbs that I have started to grow. It took me a while to adapt to the habit of buying seasonally, but it's certainly starting to pay off. I have learned from the less-than-successful stories. Feel free to laugh at my errors while making sure you don't do the same.

Before reading this book, you may have been under the impression that dehydrating food was about making a few vegetable chips and beef jerky. As we reach the end, you can now see the true extent of what you can achieve in a fun and creative way. I have one more hope, to encourage other people to join the dehydrating food adventure and reap the rewards. You can help with this. If I could ask a small favor, for you to leave a review on Amazon, others can see that drying their own foods is within their abilities and worth their while.

There is only one thing left to do and that's to start dehydrating. You have templates for plans and charts to get you going. Start with something as simple as thinking about the last meal you had. What ingredients could you have dehydrated to make the meal healthier? Take a look in your cupboards and fridge. What will spoil soon? These are the perfect places to start, and there is no better time than now. Good luck—I'm rooting for you!

REFERENCES

Alfaro, Danilo. 2019. "Moist Heat Cooking Methods." The Spruce Eats. July 12, 2019. https://www.thespruceeats.com/moist-heat-cooking-methods-a2-995848

"Ann Wigmore Quotes (Author of the Wheatgrass Book)." n.d. https://www.goodreads.com/author/quotes/385454.Ann_Wigmore

Appleton, Jeremy. 2018. "The Gut-Brain Axis: Influence of Microbiota on Mood and Mental Health." NIH. August 2018. https://www.ncbi.nlm.nih.gov/pmc/articles/PMC6469458/

Aubrey, Allison. 2022. "The U.S. Diet Is Deadly. Here Are 7 Ideas to Get Americans Eating Healthier." *NPR*, August 31, 2022. https://www.npr.org/sections/health-shots/2022/08/31/1120004717/the-u-s-diet-is-deadly-here-are-7-ideas-to-get-americans-eating-healthier

Backpacking Chef. n.d. "How to Store Dehydrated Food for Backpacking and Emergency." https://www.backpackingchef.com/vacuum-seal-bags.html

Baldwin, Darcy. 2024. "Cosori Food Dehydrator Reviews." The Purposeful Pantry. June 8, 2024. https://www.thepurposefulpantry.com/cosori/

Baranda, Ana. n.d. "Why Is It Important to Consum Seasonal Food? Here are four reasons." AZTI. https://www.azti.es/en/why-is-it-important-to-consum-seasonal-food

Best Buy. n.d. *Gourmia - 6-Tray Food Dehydrator - Black. Best Buy.* https://www.bestbuy.com/site/gourmia-6-tray-food-dehydrator-black/6157200.p?skuId=6157200&intl=nosplash

Brod & Taylor. n.d. "Sahara Folding Dehydrator." https://brodandtaylor.com/products/sahara-folding-dehydrator?variant=37376502956188

CDC. n.d. "About Trichinellosis." CDC Trichinosis. https://www.cdc.gov/trichinellosis/about/index.html

Chrissy. 2024. "31 Inspirational Self Care Quotes You'Re Going to Love." *Organise My House* (blog). June 16, 2024. https://organisemyhouse.com/inspirational-self-care-quotes/

Cliff, Cathy. 2022. "How Bad Is Ultra-processed Food for the Climate, Nature and Health?" August 24, 2022. https://www.soilassociation.org/blogs/2022/august/24/how-bad-is-ultra-processed-food-for-the-planet/

Colangelo, Harmony. 2023. "The World's Oldest Jar of Honey Is From 3500 BC." Tasting Table. March 3, 2023. https://www.tastingtable.com/1216602/the-worlds-oldest-jar-of-honey-is-from-3500-bc/

Cutler's. n.d. "Cuisinart 5-Tray Food Dehydrator - Cutler'S Cuisinart Food Dehydrator." https://cutlersonline.com/product/cuisinart-5-tray-food-dehydrator/

Dahl, Danielle. 2024. "139 Cooking Quotes That Will Entice Your Inner Chef." Everyday Power. January 21, 2024. https://everydaypower.com/cooking-quotes/

Dehydrated Foodz. 2024. "The Impact of Dehydrator Usage on Your Electricity Bills." *LinkedIn.* https://www.linkedin.com/pulse/impact-dehydrator-usage-your-electricity-bills-dehydrated-foodz-xkdxe/

Digital. 2024. "Taboo World of Food Wastage." Delta Corporation Limited. July 4, 2024. https://delta.co.zw/taboo-world-of-food-wastage/

Eartheasy. n.d. "Excalibur 3900 Deluxe Series Food Dehydrator - 9 Tray." https://eartheasy.com/excalibur-3900-deluxe-series-food-dehydrator-9-tray/#reviews_pro

Elite Gourmet. n.d. "5 Tier Food Dehydrator With Adjustable Temperature Controls." Shop Elite Gourmet - Small Kitchen Appliances. https://shopelitegourmet.com/products/elite-gourmet-5-tier-food-dehydrator-efd319?variant=41689008111774

Englert, Jonathan. 2024. "The Cost of Food Waste Globally Is Staggering; We Can All Do Our Part to Help." Good & Fugly. April 12, 2024. https://goodandfugly.com.au/blogs/news/the-cost-of-food-waste-globally-is-staggering-we-can-all-do-our-part-to-help

Environmental Protection Agency. 2024. "Sustainable Management of Food Basics." US EPA. October 10, 2024. https://www.epa.gov/sustainable-management-food/sustainable-management-food-basics

Environmental Working Group. 2024. "The Dirty Dozen." EWG. 2024. https://www.ewg.org/foodnews/dirty-dozen.php

"Excalibur Nourish Life." 2014. *Excalibur.* https://housewares.blob.core.windows.net/exhdir/original/catalog/5edc9eac-d7dc-4b52-8534-85e8a667a4c3.pdf

Food Safety and Inspection Service. 2024. "High Altitude Cooking." August 13, 2024. https://www.fsis.usda.gov/food-safety/safe-food-handling-and-preparation/food-safety-basics/high-altitude-cooking

Foodwise. n.d. "How Far Does Your Food Travel to Get to Your Plate?: Foodwise." https://foodwise.org/learn/how-far-does-your-food-travel-to-get-to-your-plate/

Haytowitz, David B., and Seema Bhagwat. 2010. "USDA Database for the Oxygen Radical Absorbance Capacity (ORAC) of Selected Foods, Release 2." *Supperberries.Com.* https://www.superberries.com/assets/images/PDFs/ORAC_R2Fruit-Vegetables2010.pdf

Healthy Instant Pot. n.d. "Healthy Instant Pot Recipes." Healthy Instant Pot Recipes. https://www.healthyinstantpotrecipes.com/about/

Hegerfeld-Baker, Joan. n.d. "Dehydrating Foods." Kansas State University. https://cottonwood.k-state.edu/health-nutrition/dehydratign_foods.html

Hodgens, Barb. n.d. "Dehydrating Fruit Pretreatment & Drying Times + Chart." Luvele ES. https://www.luvele.es/blogs/recipe-blog/dehydrating-fruit-pretreatment-drying-times-chart?srsltid=AfmBOoqF5vnuQJNjVDSmGSEJbJnxTaZRD Jai4XSyBupcdUJW-QSmVPNk

Huffstetler, Erin. n.d. "Learn How to Store Home-Dried Foods." The Spruce Eats. https://www.thespruceeats.com/how-to-store-home-dried-foods-1388331

Inbound Pursuit. 2024. "How Long to Marinate Jerky." *Mahogany Smoked Meats* (blog). April 10, 2024. https://smokedmeats.com/blogs/news/how-long-to-marinate-jerky

Inverclyde Council. 2020. "Wondering What Foods Are in Season this Month?" *X (Formerly Twitter)*. https://x.com/inverclyde/status/1245316249535610880

Jakubiec, Cindy. 2023. "How The American Diet Has Been Weaponized for Mass Destruction." Anchored in Health. February 12, 2023. https://drcindyjakubiec.com/how-the-american-diet-has-been-weaponized-for-mass-destruction

Kohli, Rajnit. 2018. "Dehydrated Marinade for Meats and Vegetables Used as a Natural Flavour Enhancer." *ResearchGate*, September. https://www.researchgate.net/publication/327418307_Dehydrated_Marinade_For_Meats_and_Vegetables_used_as_a_natural_flavour_enhancer

LaBorde, Luke, PhD. 2023. "Let's Preserve: Drying Fruits and Vegetables (Dehydration)." April 13, 2023. https://extension.psu.edu/lets-preserve-drying-fruits-and-vegetables-dehydration

Lang, Ariane. 2024. "How Does Freeze-Drying Work and Are Freeze-Dried Foods Healthy?" Healthline. January 30, 2024. https://www.healthline.com/nutrition/freeze-drying

Le Cordon Bleu. n.d. "One Trick Which Makes Good Fermented Vegetables Great." https://www.cordonbleu.edu/news/art-of-fermentation-one-trick-to-make-fermented-vegetables-great/

London, Lela. 2023. "Can You Eat Yourself Drunk?" VICE. June 6, 2023. https://www.vice.com/en/article/can-you-eat-yourself-drunk/

"Mahatma Gandhi Quote." n.d. A-Z Quotes. https://www.azquotes.com/quote/538974

Marsh, Jacob. 2023. "How Many Watt Does an Electric Oven Use?" EnergySage. December 6, 2023. https://www.energysage.com/electricity/house-watts/how-many-watts-does-an-electric-oven-and-stove-use/

Medindia. 2020. "Antioxidant Food Chart - Spices and Herbs." October 20, 2020. https://www.medindia.net/patients/calculators/antioxidant-food-chart-spices-and-herbs.asp

Melynn, Katie. 2023. "NESCO FD-1040 Gardenmaster Digital Pro Dehydrator Review." The Spruce Eats. September 21, 2023. https://www.thespruceeats.com/nesco-fd-1040-dehydrator-review-4769933#toc-features-top-of-the-line

Mitchell & Cooper. n.d. "What Is a Dehydrator & How Can They Be Used? A Commercial Buying Guide." https://www.mitchellcooper.co.uk/what-is-a-dehy drator-commercial-buying-guide

Modernist Cuisine. 2013. "The Maillard Reaction." March 20, 2013. https://modernistcuisine.com/mc/the-maillard-reaction/

NASA. n.d. "Ocean Warming." Climate NASA. https://climate.nasa.gov/vital-signs/ocean-warming/?intent=121

Naturis. 2024. "3 Global Trends for 2024 Highlighting the Shift to Healthy Food - Naturis." Naturis. May 28, 2024. https://naturis.com/3-global-trends-for-2024-highlighting-the-shift-to-healthy-food/

Newman, Tim, and Kenji Morimoto. 2024. "How to Ferment at Home: A Simple Guide." March 13, 2024. https://zoe.com/learn/fermentation-101

Numanna Foundation. n.d. "The Complete History of Dehydrated Food." *Numanna* (blog). https://numanna.com/the-complete-history-of-dehydrated-food/

Nummer, Brian. n.d. "Sun Drying." Nchfp.Uga.Edu. https://nchfp.uga.edu/how/dry/drying-general/sun-drying

Outdoor Herbivore Blog. 2019. "Cooking Dries Foods at High Altitude." November 11, 2019. https://blog.outdoorherbivore.com/camp-tips/cooking-dried-foods-at-high-altitude/

Outdoor Home. n.d. "LEM Mighty Bite 5-Tray Countertop Dehydrator 1152." https://outdoorhome.com/products/mighty-bite-5-tray-countertop-dehydrator-1152?srsltid=AfmBOoqpVKzET6kRgafaTy8mEkVaC4KWffEfVP7Eqf OOT1_0BrhRJkVO

Pham-Huy, Lien Ai, Hua He, and Chuong Pham-Huy. 2008. "Free Radicals, Antioxidants in Disease and Health." NIH. June 4, 2008. https://www.ncbi.nlm.nih.gov/pmc/articles/PMC3614697/

Pick Your Own. n.d. "Food Dehydration Problems: How to Solve Food Drying Problems." https://www.pickyourown.org/dryingfoods-solving-common-problems.php

Pope, Sarah. n.d. "How to Dehydrate Food to Preserve Enzymes + Probiotics." The Healthy Home Economist. https://www.thehealthyhomeeconomist.com/how-to-dehydrate-food/

Porter, Becky. 2024. "9 Benefits of Dehydrating Food That May Surprise You." The Seasonal Homestead. May 31, 2024. https://www.theseasonalhomestead.com/9-benefits-of-dehydrating-food-that-may-surprise-you/

QuoteStats. n.d. "Top 26 Quotes About Preservatives." https://quotestats.com/topic/quotes-about-preservatives/

Raging Bull. n.d. "What Is Jerky? 10 Facts About Jerky." *Raging Bull Snacks* (blog). https://ragingbullsnacks.com/what-is-jerky-everything-you-need-to-know/

Royaluxkitchen. n.d. "Magic Mill Food Dehydrator Machine MFD-7700." https://magicmillusa.com/products/magic-mill-food-dehydrator-machine-mfd-7700

Seaver, Victoria Seaver. 2023. "Here's Why You Get an Orange in Your Christmas Stocking." *EatingWell*, July 10, 2023. https://www.eatingwell.com/article/7873163/orange-in-christmas-stocking

Sedano, Isabela. 2024. "35 Food Waste Quotes Encouraging Changing Food Habits." TRVST. April 8, 2024. https://www.trvst.world/waste-recycling/food-waste/food-waste-quotes/

STPA Forestwood. 2020. "Overcoming Adversity." Something to Ponder About. June 15, 2020. https://forestwoodfolkart.wordpress.com/2020/06/15/overcoming-adversity/

Terry, Natalie, and Kara Gross Margolis. 2017. "Serotonergic Mechanisms Regulating the GI Tract: Experimental Evidence and Therapeutic Relevance." NIH. July 25, 2017. https://www.ncbi.nlm.nih.gov/pmc/articles/PMC5526216

The Craft Patch. n.d. "Glass Etching: Everything You Need to Know." https://www.thecraftpatchblog.com/glass-etching/

"Tony Horton Quote." n.d. A-Z Quotes. https://www.azquotes.com/quote/814717

Total Vet. 2024. "The Rising Cost of Dog Food." July 25, 2024. https://total.vet/the-rising-cost-of-dog-food/

Tribest. n.d. "Sedona® Express Food Dehydrator With Stainless Steel Trays." https://tribest.com/products/sedona-express-sde-s6780-b?srsltid=AfmBOoqIherG4j3xQKtS4E2bxUxxIe4cCroBE2LgCNJkPeeXfKW1gjc9

University of Minnesota Extension. 1993. "How to Blanch Vegetables Before Preserving." UMN Extension. 1993. https://extension.umn.edu/preserving-and-preparing/vegetable-blanching-directions-and-times-home-freezer-storage

US. Foods. n.d. "Seasonal Produce Guide." *Usfoods*. https://www.usfoods.com/content/dam/usf/pdf/produce/Freshness-Guide.pdf

USU Extension. n.d. "Freeze Drying: Essential and Nice-to-have Tools and Supplies." USU. https://extension.usu.edu/preserve-the-harvest/research/freeze-drying-essential-and-nice-to-have-tools-and-supplies

VacPac. 2023. "Top 15 Benefits of Vacuum Sealing Your Food." VACPAC. July 31, 2023. https://www.vacpac.com.au/top-15-benefits-of-vacuum-sealing-your-food-2/

Valeii, Kathi. 2024. "Phytic Acid Benefits, Health Concerns, and Food Sources." Verywell Health. September 22, 2024. https://www.verywellhealth.com/phytic-acid-5088824

Valley Food Storage. 2023. "The Shelf Life of Dehydrated Foods: How Long Can Dehydrated Food Last?" *Valley Food Storage*(blog). July 12, 2023. https://valleyfoodstorage.com/blogs/inside-vfs/how-long-does-dehydrated-food-last?srsltid=AfmBOoryVjWHh709Ky8EF

Warrell, Ellen. 2023. "How Does Processed Food Harm the Environment? - Wicked Leeks." Wicked Leeks. February 28, 2023. https://wickedleeks.riverford.co.uk/features/how-does-processed-food-harm-the-environment/

WebMD. 2022. "Dehydrating Food: Is It Good for You?" November 29, 2022. https://www.webmd.com/diet/dehydrating-food-good-for-you

Wonderland Guides. 2016. "Food Dehydrating 101." May 12, 2016. https://www.wonderlandguides.com/backcountry-cooking/dehydrating-food/food-dehydrating-101